PRAISE FOR *The Woodstock Flan*

"For almost fifty years Michael Perkins has been quietly documenting your life. My life. And the lives of so many of us who live, work, or come to play in Woodstock. He's an insidious snoop. He is also one of Woodstock's greatest treasures.

"This collection of Michael's work will make you laugh, make you gasp, and make you feel warm all over, longing for times gone by, people passed, and pleasures lost.

"PS: Don't be surprised if you find yourself making a cameo appearance somewhere in the book."

—Marshall Karp,
#1 *New York Times* bestselling author
and huge Michael Perkins fan

"I should be talking about the fascinating portraits of the men and women who made Woodstock what it is, that Michael Perkins writes with authority and wit, that the reader will feel the physical beauty of this very particular village, and understand the part it has played in American history. But I find myself wanting to say, indeed, shout—that Micheal Perkins is the heart and soul of Woodstock, that he is a national treasure, and that you will find yourself falling in love with with him as so many admirers have, and as I did. Read this marvelous book and rejoice."

—Abigail Thomas, *A Three Dog Life*

"Michael Perkins's Flaneur columns from the *Woodstock Times* are masterpieces of tender wickedness, bringing us the news from Tinker Street and the great Ashokanite Republic in dispatches as wittily gossipy as they are moving and profound."

—James Lasdun, *The Fall Guy*

"These essays by the peerless poet, philosopher, and rustic flaneur Michael Perkins delve deeply, but with lightness and grace, into the heart and soul of his beloved Woodstock. Rarely has a small town with such large (some might say grandiose) ambitions been so lucky as to have a chronicler of this caliber—unfailingly faithful, unflaggingly generous, and unceasingly attentive to every quirk and quiddity of its all-too-human topography. If you want the perfect counterpart to the 'official' history of Woodstock, this is the book for you."

—Mikhail Horowitz, *Rafting into the Afterlife*

"Michael Perkins has written a vivid collection of personal stories from his forty years living in Woodstock, New York. He writes that although he can vouch for the authenticity of these true stories, he chooses to call himself, 'a mere onlooker to life, a flaneur.' Since the flaneur is a person with no business to conduct, no trains to catch, an idle stroller, with time to truly observe what is going on, he lives in the present moment, creating, recreating right now. In these exceptional stories, there is an open, natural space which encourages questioning, disagreement/agreement, dialogue, listening to the voices and stories of others, including encounters with flies, dogs, mountain talk, best friends and strangers. This is a book to read at any time, at this time."

—Gioia Timpanelli, *Sometimes the Soul: Two Novellas of Sicily*

"Michael Perkins's *The Woodstock Flaneur* is one of those books you carry around with you everywhere you go—this brilliant personal history of post-1969 festival Woodstock is also a handbook for honest living in these duplicitous times."

—Michael Hunt, President of Friends of the Library

The Woodstock Flaneur

The Woodstock Flaneur

**A SAUNTERER'S INTIMATE PORTRAIT OF
THE WORLD'S MOST FAMOUS SMALL TOWN**

MICHAEL PERKINS

ACKNOWLEDGMENTS

These pieces first appeared in the *Woodstock Times*.

The Woodstock Flaneur: A Saunterer's Intimate Portrait of the World's Most Famous Small Town. Copyright ©2018 by Michael Perkins.

Published by Bushwhack Books
www.bushwhackbooks.com

Printed in the United States of America

Library of Congress Cataloging-in-Publication Data

Perkins, Michael.

The Woodstock Flaneur : A Saunterer's Intimate Portrait of the World's Most Famous Small Town / Michael Perkins.

[Woodstock, NY] : Bushwhack Books, 2018.

184 p. ; 1.16 cm.

ISBN: 978-09886398-5-0

1. Woodstock (N.Y.) - History. 2. American Essays - 21st Century - Essays - Nonfiction - Local. 3. Woodstock (N.Y.) - Guidebooks. 4. Walking - New York (State) - Ulster County - Guidebooks.

973.734

F129 .W85

Illustrations by Carol Zaloom
Author photograph by Roy Gumpel
Cover, Ashokan map & book design by Melissa Mykal Batalin

To my friend, Will Nixon,
whose intelligence, imagination,
and hard work helped transform
a dream into this reality.

Contents

THE REPUBLIC OF ASHOKAN

1. Overlook Trail

2. Woodstock Byrdcliffe Guild

3. Artists Cemetery

4. Woodstock Cemetery

5. The Woodstock Library
   & The Village Green

6. Comeau Property

7. Woodstock Center
   for Photography

8. Mower's Market

9. The Flaneur's Home

10. Ashokan Resevoir

⊞ ⊞ ⊞ ⊞ ⊞

The Woodstock Flaneur

⊞ ⊞ ⊞ ⊞ ⊞

THIS IS A COLLECTION of true stories about people living in a small town over the past forty years. The people are artists. The town is Woodstock, New York, often called the most famous small town in the world, because of a 1969 rock festival that didn't happen here. What did happen at the start of the last century was an art colony to which interesting people were drawn. They still are.

The author of these stories can vouch for their authenticity, because he knew the people, and was often involved in what happened to them. Yet he chooses to call himself a mere onlooker to life, a flaneur. (This is a French concept, not widely known in America. Manhattan has no flaneur—yet. But Woodstock does.)

What is a flaneur?

In a world dedicated to speed and planned obsolescence, the flaneur puts on the brakes. He is an idler, an observer, who keeps moving in public just fast enough to avoid a charge of loitering or aggravated mopery. Having put his hiking boots away until he can climb in the Delectable Mountains, the flaneur's self-appointed mission is to saunter Woodstock's roads, mixing with crowds, looking and remembering four decades of living it up. He notes the passing of seasons, and the passage of citizens high and low. He recalls the layers of local history buried under the imperative of progress. He digs up secrets, remembers the forgotten, and pays last respects.

Some may understand the flaneur as being like a town historian, although he is not that; others, less kind, may think of him as a street person, a bum.

The flaneur in Woodstock believes that the patch of Catskill earth he stands on is a fine platform for observing the universe. He is a patriot of his watershed and bioregion, a citizen of Ashokan by dint of residence and exploration. He believes that by writing about Woodstock he is doing his best to encourage a sense of community in its citizens.

Stroller, dandy, saunterer, idler, man of the crowd: the flaneur is the collector of detail and its connoisseur. He is a sensibility more than an intelligence. His antecedents are literary – which may help explain his obscurity. His progenitor was Edgar Allan Poe, his midwife Charles Baudelaire; Walter Benjamin added a birth certificate in two volumes. The American novelist Edmund White is the flaneur of Paris. Other flaneurs will follow as our world speeds to its final resolution, but for now it seems right that Paris and Woodstock should have more than fame in common: writers who share the secrets of invisible cities.

A Throne on
the Village Green

THE FLANEUR'S VOCATION is to pay attention to that which is overlooked. This includes the inspection of snowstorms, peering into shop windows, saying hello to strangers, and welcoming spring. Other items in his portfolio: remembering what things used to look like, memorializing citizens who have passed on, and wondering where the hell the time has gone. If he is feeling particularly ambitious, it is within his purview to obambulate down Tinker Street keeping one eye peeled for an honest man.

All this responsibility can tire one out. The flaneur knows that to sit after a good walk is royal, even if his throne is a hard green wooden bench on a snowy early spring Village Green. He remembers seeing Paul Newman (with a beer in a bag) sitting on this throne in the eighties, when Joanne Woodward was playing in Chekhov in a River Arts production at the Byrdcliffe Theater. A royal precedent.

The Green (or should it be called "The Village Stone" in honor of its lithic renovation?) has been the symbolic heart of Woodstock for well over two centuries. The flag flies here, waving proudly in a stiff breeze, its chain clanking, Wannabe Dylans serenade the tourists. Women in Black stand in silent, unavailing protest (thus far) against the Perpetual War Machine. And the Trailways bus stops here, bringing the huddled masses yearning to breathe free up from Manhattan. (In the sixies the bus brought hippies, who were met by the local constable and put on the next bus home.)

The history of the Green is well known to the flaneur. If he closes his eyes, he can view a slide show of images mixed from his own memories and his informed imagination of the historical past—in which a parade of Lenni-Lenape, settlers, bluestone quarry workers, Irish laborers, artists, hippies and tourists march past his throne. He wonders what the first house in the hamlet looked like. Built in 1777, the Newkirk House stood near where the Chamber of Commerce booth is now. A blue historical marker memorializes it.

He opens his eyes and surveys the buildings that surround the Green; its owner, The Dutch Reformed Church, is the most prominent. He thinks it probably the most beautiful building in town. (He has never before noticed the weather vane on the top of the steeple.) Dutch settlers purchased the land now known as the Green in 1805, but had built the first church elsewhere in 1799. In 1827 the congregation held its first services in the new church. To the north sits the Charles Krack house, with its second-story veranda, where The Garden Café rubs shoulders with one of Woodstock's ubiquitous realty offices. He remembers seeing blues great Muddy Waters posing for photos in front of the building, as did Bob Dylan. H. Houst & Son has occupied the corner across Tinker Street since 1932. Down Mill Hill Road a bit, Landau Grill offers food and revivifying beverages. All of this beneath the noble brow of Overlook, which dominates the village. (He wonders how many people look up to their range of mother mountains.)

A church, a store, a tavern—presto: civilization. He remembers Jean Turmo's as The News Shop, where he could get an ice cream cone, a hot dog, or a bus ticket, and buy a newspaper. In the eighties traffic was so light that when the flaneur went for a Sunday *Times* he found a nonchalant dog sleeping in the street. Oriole 9 is in the building once occupied by Mower's, where you could run a tab on groceries, and have them delivered.

The flaneur's reverie is interrupted by the appearance of a familiar figure talking loudly to himself. It is the lean, bearded street Bedouin known as Jogger John. Call him Biker John now. Whereas he used to run everywhere like an electric bunny, age has slowed John's pace a tad and put him on wheels. On this cold morning, he has come to sweep the Green where the snow has melted, and to dispense advice. He always says something you haven't heard before.

John's presence reminds the flaneur of two absences: Mark and Lincoln. Mark Rogosin, also known as Silent Mark, who later died in a nursing home, was a familiar sight on the Green and in front of CVS. He would stand for hours in silent witness, sometimes giving the thumbs-up sign. Lincoln Woodrow Wilson Jr.'s death came more recently.

The flaneur has fond memories of both men. Mark had been a patent attorney, the owner of a Fifth Avenue apartment, who traveled the world. In Woodstock he became known for digging a great hole and giving rocks painted with "Om"s to people he liked.

Lincoln drove an old telephone van, and sometimes gave the flaneur a ride when he was not walking Ohayo Mountain Road himself. Lincoln was a voluble exponent of esoteric health-food remedies, some of which he believed would cure his cancer. RIP, Lincoln.

Traffic flows past the Green in never-ending ripples. The flaneur watches it, looking for people he knows. Walking on the road, he cannot see through windshields; now he recognizes people's faces. Sometimes they wave.

An orange Town of Woodstock pickup truck drives slowly past. At the wheel is Ray Brundage, a handsome straight shooter who is head of the Maintenance Department. The flaneur has found his honest man.

Then another honest man appears, a thin, older cat on an antique bicycle. It is Michael Esposito, West Point born musician, *Woodstock Times* cartoonist, and bike doctor.

Then there is a third: Big Paul Nelson, the Woodstock Library's resident philosopher. As with Kant in Königsberg, you can set your watch by his walk to the Library.

For the first time, the flaneur notices the Peace Pole on the Green. It wishes us "Peace on Earth" in a hundred languages. If a spacecraft should land on the Green, perhaps our visitors will recognize Latvian rather than English. The pole was built by Jesse (Santa Claus) Reimer.

The noon sun is weak. To warm up, the flaneur decides to pace the circumference of the oval island that is the Green. It takes him a hundred-and-seventy steps to walk around it, and seventy-five steps to cross it.

Spring will bring the flowerbeds to vivid life. The gardeners make them more beautiful each year.

He thinks for a moment of the Green as an island, and himself as Robinson Crusoe. In a world based on the wheel, the Green is surrounded by a surging sea of automobiles.

The Trailways bus pulls up, and passengers climb down stiffly, as if from a stagecoach in a Western movie.

The flaneur recalls his many arrivals on the Green. Once, after a month in Europe, when he stepped down onto the Green he felt a crazy, irresistible impulse to kneel and kiss the stones of home.

Now he stands up, refreshed, ready to continue his leisurely stroll down Tinker Street, looking for signs of spring.

The Woodstock Library
—A Sexton's Report

THE FIRST TIME the flaneur saw the Woodstock Library, it appeared almost like a ghost ship, illumined by shafts of sunlight, out of a wintry fog. He stood transfixed, watching as the fog blew off. The mountains that loom over the village had white beards. A snowstorm the day before had closed Tinker Street. The only sound was snow removal scraping on the road. Drawn by the library, he crunched across the crust of snow that covered its great lawn, headed toward his destiny.

It was January 1972, and after a decade in the Empire City, he had come to Woodstock in search of a life not ruled by money. So he was at liberty, so to speak, when he entered the library.

A woman who might have been a double for the Wicked Witch of the West in the Wizard of Oz sat reading at the circulation desk. He introduced himself, and told her he wanted a library card. Her name was Ellen Roberts, and she had spent her life in publishing before becoming a small town librarian. They chatted for a long time in the empty library. She told him she and her husband Dick—

he was a writer who had sold a western to the movies—raised African lion hunting dogs, Rhodesian Ridgebacks. It was a happy encounter. There was no sign that thirteen years later he would become the unacknowledged sexton of this holy place.

The flaneur did not use words like "holy" lightly, but he had seen enough of churches and libraries to feel more reverence for the latter. Libraries were democratic, nondenominational, and noncommercial, open to all without exception, storehouses of knowledge and literature, places for learning and growth: the cultural center of any community.

Heaven, he often thought, was a small-town library. But heavens must be propped up by willing hands. If he wanted to partake of paradise, he saw that he must earn it. So he began serving the library on various committees, becoming a trustee in 1985 and starting the Library Forum the next year. (The forum is the library's most popular outreach program for adults, and the longest-running forum in the Hudson Valley.)

Ellen Roberts made herself so disliked by the community (she did not suffer fools gladly, a type of sufferance essential to survival in Woodstock) that she was replaced as librarian by children's librarian D.J. Stern, a friend of the flaneur's who asked him to become Director of the annual Library Fair, a position he held for eighteen years. The flaneur's involvement became close to obsessive when Stern asked him to become the building manager. With a staff of one, and with D.J.'s encouragement and support, the flaneur served as the library's sexton for nearly ten years, attempting to give the town the library it paid for.

A church sexton took care of a church, inside and out; rang its bells and buried its dead. The flaneur approached his job as sexton with equivalent seriousness. He shoveled snow, swept the parking lot, had roofs repaired and rooms painted. He learned to deal with all aspects of maintenance problems, but he also slowly added comforts, like a full-sized refrigerator, new blinds, central AC, and new carpeting. He served on committees, and recruited new trustees. There was more, but the flaneur lacks the chops to toot his own horn. "Fools' names and fools' faces are often seen in public places," he would reply, when asked to do more than write about what he saw. He listed his good deeds—if such they were—to establish his credibility. When it came to the library, he knew whereof he spoke.

D.J. retired, having made indelible contributions to the library. The flaneur ceased being sexton. Amy Raff became Director, and set her own ambitious agenda. She seemed destined to go from one success to the next. But trouble came instead, and she quit.

What was difficult for a cynical old curmudgeon like the flaneur, battle hardened in a half dozen of Woodstock's teapot tempests, to grok without gagging, was why the Annex War had started. Surely so much bad cess could not be over aesthetics. Why, the flaneur asked himself, were cooperation and compromise dirty words in his beloved hometown?

The flaneur loves libraries, and books, and, it follows, people who love books. Like everyone with eyes to see, he knows that he lives in Paradise, here and now. He knows the reality of hell because he once took a long ride through it. "But nothing comes without a fight," he reminded himself. "And nothing good remains that way for long, unless it's guarded."

Library patrons fell into various categories. The most challenging were the homeless—unmoored, leaky boats in choppy waters. The library was their only port in a storm, and when winter came, a few sat in the reading room, all possessions in shopping bags under the table. Some were smelly. When people complained, the librarian explained to them that the courts had ruled that the homeless could not be barred. They came to be called the "Library Pets." They were poor, hungry, and—an assessment, not a judgment—significantly loony: a sweet paranoid schizophrenic, a young man with an obsessive-compulsive disorder that made it difficult for him to cross thresholds without a lengthy counting ritual; to be behind him leaving the library was to be late for your next appointment. The most notable pet had, like Diogenes, chosen destitution. Mark, a former attorney, was friends with the librarian and the flaneur, and had been given the freedom to use her office. If he liked you he painted a symbol on a rock, and gave it to you.

The flaneur found it difficult to explain to visitors what made the Woodstock Library different from other libraries, but perhaps he came closest when he said that it was classless—that it really was for everyone. Even canine companions were admitted.

The Ghosts of Mill Hill Road

THE DAY AFTER the first snowfall in December the sun came out, and everything sparkled the way it did when the flaneur first arrived in Woodstock in 1972. He was thirty, and the sixties had sped him from Ohio to New York to this village he would come to both love and hate—like any true Woodstocker. But then he thought he was just visiting.

He stayed. The years roared by. He hiked through his life with great strides.

But, sooner or later, life forces everyone to slow down. For him, the brakes were put on when he took a serious fall one March day at Kaaterskill Falls. He went from being a long-distance walker to a new life as a saunterer, a stroller on village roads.

The French call this type of walker a flaneur. The flaneur is so attracted to the street he's walked a thousand times that he sees with X-ray vision through the palimpsest created by transformations. He sees through time as well as space.

When he arrived in 1972, today's Tinker Street merchants were young hippie entrepreneurs. Everyone drove junkers. Some winter days the town was so empty and the traffic so minimal that dogs slept in the middle of the street. There seemed to be only one cop in town—Lud Baumgarten—and he was a police force unto himself. The music scene was huge.

The flaneur, as he idles from the Village Green—now the Village Stone—to his destination at Woodstock Physical Therapy on Route 212, remembers an extraordinary cast of characters. Most of them are dead now; they are shades, but he hears them call. He remembers their stories.

He pauses before the Landau Grill and it becomes again the Pub, an Irish bar presided over by a white-haired Spencer Tracy named Patrick, who served strong ale to old newspapermen like Sid Kline, a former editor. Sid and his cronies would discuss literary questions like Joyce scholars, and wager on who could identify the Seven Wonders of the Ancient World. One of Woodstock's finest painters, Paul Naylor, lived upstairs.

Down the road the pizza parlor draws the flaneur's attention. Thirty-eight years ago, it was Ken's Exxon, owned by gruff Ken Reynolds, who single-handedly (well, he had Joe Clark and many other mechanics working for him) kept the village's Ford Falcons and Dodge Darts running. Ken was the kind of guy who would bring his wrecker out in a snowstorm to haul you out of a ditch, then growl "aw, forget it" when you tried to pay him. Ken's wife Dodie tried valiantly to collect the bills.

Across the street was Dot's—or Duey's—the Bread Alone café of the day. Up the road at Deming Street was The Joyous Lake, called by some "The Joyless Fake." Nevertheless, Ron Merian's wife Valma (their daughter was named Three) presented all the great music of that era. One night Maria Muldaur brought down the house with her hit, "Midnight at the Oasis." The food was good, the bar was hand carved, and life was governed by the I Ching.

Across Deming Street was Deanie's, the real Woodstock watering hole. It featured mediocre but reliable food and an atmosphere unpretentiously comfortable. One night the flaneur was sitting with his editor when Mary Ellen van Wagenen, a waitress, told him his house on Calamar Lane was on fire. He ran all the way home down Tinker Street. Some kids had been playing with matches. Not long after, Deanie's burned.

In Castaways, across the street from Catskill Art Supply, was a hippie television station. There the erotic novelist and erstwhile philosopher Marco Vassi and Evelyn Honig, with others, created Meta-Monkey Video. There was a news program nightly. The flaneur gave the latest update on the English language. A little later the notorious tattoo artist Spider Webb opened a studio there.

Picking his way carefully along Mill Hill, the flaneur passes Bradley Meadows without pause, rambles past the rebuilt Woodstock Playhouse, and comes to Cucina. This building was Deanie's last stand, where Margaret played the piano, a nude hung above the bar, and everybody who was anybody showed up sooner or later. The most beautiful woman in Woodstock, Freya DeNitto, waitressed there. One evening Freya had just served on the porch, and the flaneur went to the facilities.

He opened the front door to encounter a huge, familiar-looking drunk coming at him. He thought, this must be an hallucination. The man looked like Liberty Valance.

It was. Lee Marvin, who played the title character in the great John Ford film, was a Woodstock native. There he was, as big in life as on the screen. The flaneur got out of his way. (He found out later that Marvin had offered to buy a round for all his friends at the bar. When the check came, the cowboy pulled out a thousand dollar bill. Since Deanie's couldn't cash it, he smiled—and walked.)

The flaneur shakes his head and walks carefully, facing traffic, past the golf course. The sun is high and in his eyes, and the traffic is relentless. He reminds himself that he dislikes nostalgia, but he recalls William Faulkner's words: "The past is never dead. It's not even past."

🏵 🏵 🏵 🏵 🏵

Celebration!

🏵 🏵 🏵 🏵 🏵

Ed Balmer

TO PARAPHRASE AUNTIE MAME, "life is a party and most poor suckers don't know how to celebrate." The flaneur liked to think of parties as group expressions of gratitude for being alive—like prayer, but with music. Although he doesn't look the type to party hearty—he is old, cadaverous, bent, and of mournful mien—the flaneur is, withal, a party animal. The list of parties he has attended or thrown constitute an autobiography of celebration from initiation, at eleven, to his biggest, the two-week Woodstock Bicentennial Celebration. The flaneur had learned from these one of life's great secrets: how to have a good time. Bop till you drop.

Beatrice was his guide through the social intricacies of his first party. He was new in the neighborhood, and one warm Saturday he noticed her on the street in tight white shorts that showed off the deep brown tan of her legs to wicked advantage.

Despite his shyness, he spoke to her. The next day she invited him to her birthday party, at which spin the bottle was played. He went into the closet with Beatrice reluctantly, as boys will, and emerged a young man with a new spring in his step.

In his first years in New York, the flaneur saw every kind of party, and soon wearied of gatherings that were not truly social, but another category of work, eased somewhat by white wine and nibbles. These occasions were seldom celebratory. Those he spoke to were anxious to find a date, status, or relief from boredom. The flaneur wanted more. So he decided to find a place where people still knew the value of "wasting time," and play.

He took a bus to Woodstock on a crisp October day when the autumn leaves were still turning, and saw, when the bus stopped at the Village Green, that he had arrived at the Right Place. People had gathered around a man who was talking loudly while operating an old-fashioned cider press, and giving out free cups of his pulpy product. The flaneur thought the man looked interesting, like he might have some mischief in his pockets. Like many country men, he wore a sheath knife on his belt, which he used to cut a slice of tart apple for the stranger off the noon bus. They fell to talking about apples, and when they finished pressing the last batch, the flaneur helped the man and his two kids load the apple press into the back of a pickup that had seen better days when Lassie was a pup. The man grinned.

"You like parties? We have venison, cold beer, and hot music." And that was how he met a true Woodstock character, Ed Balmer.

The Balmer homestead's backyard was a great lawn decorated with sculptures made of rusting Detroit iron. Some still ran. The lawn was suffused with soft autumn light, filtered through outstretched arboreal arms that welcomed a greater variety of people than those he saw at New York parties. They strolled on the freshly cut grass laughing and sipping fresh cider. In years to come, the flaneur would measure other parties by this celebration of the apple harvest.

There were so many parties... at first, missing his city friends, he would invite them to a house party to celebrate birthdays. Friends, good talk, wine, and dancing: celebration.

The flaneur could not dance—except for the horizontal mambo—but he loved to do what his friend Melvin Van Peebles mocked as the "White Man's Shuffle." He also liked art openings in the seventies in Woodstock, before conversation degenerated to mindless talk about computers, and art faded into technology.

The Beaux Arts Ball

REASONING THAT if boredom at parties was to be his lot, why not magnify the torture? On his theory that as you turn up the volume, things become more interesting, he persuaded staff at Ulster Arts magazine to revive an old Woodstock tradition—the Artists and Models Ball. And so on a mild evening in fall nearly forty years ago, five hundred people in costume showed up at the Art Students League to celebrate being artists. Two bands kept things lively, and by midnight the dance floor was wild.

The Woodstock Bicentennial Celebration

THE FLANEUR was Program Director for the Woodstock Guild in 1986 when he was assigned to serve on a committee that was to come up with plans for a Bicentennial Celebration. The committee was made up of people who liked to hear themselves talk. The flaneur is a shy guy, but he is easily bored. After listening for an hour to some good ideas buried in dense verbiage, he protested. All eyes focused on him. Before he could protest again, he was named chair of the celebration.

A year later, in spring 1987, Woodstock threw a two-week-long party for itself that everyone agreed was the best that Woodstock had seen since the Maverick festivals. Parades, concerts, exhibitions, plays—every day offered a new reason to feel good about the town. Hundreds of people worked to make it a success. Cynics said it was enough to make you believe that Santa and the tooth fairy had put happy pills in the water supply.

Ed Redux

THE FLANEUR ran into Ed Balmer at a long-ago birthday party for the poet Janine Vega. They were standing in the kitchen of a house off Tinker Street. Liquor had loosened the flaneur's tongue as he told Ed his theory about parties and celebration. He was feigning modesty as he recounted the fun he'd given people, and Ed called him on it. "You should be proud. Don't forget, it ain't braggin' if it's true."

Many Woodstocks

THE WORLD'S MOST FAMOUS SMALL TOWN exists in time as well as space. For devotees of local history, it is a vast place, with buildings superimposed upon buildings. Even now, the flaneur cannot pass the Chamber of Commerce information booth on Rock City Road without seeing, in his mind's sharp eye, the elegant Longyear House that once graced the spot. (It was demolished in the early seventies by its owner, a perfidious bank which sent bulldozers to flatten it after promising to spare it.) Those with good imaginations may be able to visualize the first building on or near that spot, a tavern. They may also be able to hear, however faintly, the ringing of the blacksmith's hammer on Mill Hill Road, and smell the ripe odors of horse apples on Tinker Street and of early industry—the tanneries on Tannery Brook, an odor so strong it could make a razorback hog gag, and crows fall from the sky.

This fourth dimension is home to the flaneur, who stopped believing in "reality" about the time he learned that a table is not solid, but a whirl of atoms. He often thought of the periods in local history he wanted to travel back in time to visit. He wanted to see the first encounter, probably at Waghkonk, now Zena, of the sturdy Dutch settlers with the small, gentle Lenni-Lenape, who had hunted beneath the magnificent shadow of Overlook for thousands of years, sheltering in nearby caves, and growing corn in the Zena cornfield. Did the natives protest this usurpation, or were they hospitable? If the corn was high, who planted it?

The invisible history of Woodstock might be tracked by such encounters, the flaneur thought—the endless conflict between newcomers and those who considered themselves natives. City dwellers who came to escape the heat (they stayed at the Riseley boarding house that is now Cucina), the artists drawn by Byrdcliffe and the Art Students League, the hippies, IBMers, the latest wave seems to be writers—successful professionals only. Woodstock has become pricey.

There are thirty-four places named Woodstock in the world. Seeing each of them was on his auxiliary bucket list. In 1987, the flaneur walked to Woodstock, Connecticut, west to east, in one week to publicize the Woodstock Bicentennial.

There is also a Woodstock, England connected to us long ago by a memorial stone in the foundation of our library. While on a walking tour of England some years back, the flaneur made a point of visiting Winston Churchill's hometown.

The road to Woodstock offers no hint of the beauty that awaits the traveler in the village. The A34 from Oxford passes enormous fields and condominium developments, and at the edge of the village stands an Esso station looking like a space station put there by aliens. The bus passes Blenheim Palace, Sir Winston Churchill's ancestral home.

Not wanting to walk A34, the flaneur has taken a bus, which stops at the Crown Inn, at the corner of Oxford and High Street, in the center of the village. It is a gray day in October, with rain threatening. A stroll down Oxford Street, which is pleasant and very old and lined with tourist shops, is sufficient to demonstrate that Woodstock is Woodstock—even if we don't speak the same language.

Here, for instance, is Bentlies of Woodstock, offering antiques and gifts, between Woodstock Turf Accountants and a fish and chips shop. Across the street stands the Woodstock Methodist church, a modest fifteenth-century pile.

And look: There is Woodstock Design, and a slew of galleries dedicated to giving people the kind of art they like. There is a fruit and vegetable stand on the corner. Hanging from hooks outside above the apples and pears are three big hares, two ducks, and four bright pheasants. Then comes Town Hall, which is exhibiting the Woodstock Festival of Decorative Art. And Woodstock Library....

There are as many Woodstocks as there are people drawn here. When the flaneur first saw his own Woodstock and the northeastern Catskill Mountains, it was love at first sight. He has walked, hiked, climbed, biked, sauntered, and even driven—mostly under duress—in this paradise, and it has never failed to refresh and renew him. Perhaps this is because of the needs he brings to it... perhaps. But the flaneur prefers to believe that there is Magic here—he prefers to believe that here the earth is alive, that spirits abound, and that this land he calls Ashokan is one of the world's sacred spots.

And if not, it will do until the real thing comes along.

Dressing Down

RECENTLY, WHILE LOOKING THROUGH a forgotten cache of old photos, the flaneur came across one that sent a pang of embarrassment through him. It was taken when he first arrived in Woodstock, back in the ganja-shrouded seventies when today's town fathers were still raising hell and dressing down.

The Polaroid showed the flaneur's youthful self togged out as a hippie—a tribe he did not cotton to. He wore bib (Osh Kosh, By Gosh) overalls. All he needed was a corncob pipe and a fiddle, and he could try out for the Grand Ole Opry. He shuddered, recalling Oscar Wilde's warning that only fools don't judge by appearances, and destroyed the evidence of his callow conformity. Bibs were fine for the farm, but....

The flaneur's image of himself was not Maynard Krebs, or even Jack Kerouac. Having grown up poor, he liked to play dress up. When he went out for a walk he saw himself as a dandy. Each of us rebels in his own way, and rather than a bandana, the flaneur wore an ascot.

The flaneur avoided the Woodstock Festival because he knew that wearing a suit would have made too much of a statement. (You couldn't go naked all the time, alas.) Imagine, then, how he must have felt strolling on Tinker Street in 1972: distinctly out of place. He would have to find a disguise—thus the bibs. He drew the line at tie-dye, but he tried a beard.

Americans have been dressing down since the sixties, when grown men took to wearing adolescent garb—jeans and ballcaps; but Woodstockers of that era tried to out do each other in sloppiness. The flaneur thought Woodstockers were just lazy, because they would show up everywhere, from candlelight concerts to outdoor weddings, dressed in denim. Such uniformity in a proudly maverick village was puzzling. (At this point, you may well ask, so what? The world has so many pressing problems, surely how we dress is unimportant. Being a polite sort, the flaneur considered this. Then he remembered grunge, and felt his spine stiffen.)

He remembered his first encounter—at the drumming circle on the Village Green—with the youthful protest of grunge. They made a fetish of egregious ugliness. He smiled at the irony of their costumes. They had adopted prison fashion—no belts or laces—in their effort to stand out as individuals. They dressed so down their oversized pants dragged on the ground, and their butt cracks showed. Their "body art," far from being tribal, looked unearned, conventional. They attracted attention, but it was pity for lost waifs that he felt. The cult of ugliness in dress, behavior, and what passes for art has ruled for decades in the art world. While intended to signify dystopian authenticity, it is in reality just another marketing trick. The kids had been conned.

Well, at least they were not wearing bib overalls, the flaneur thought. How did he want them to dress?

He was looking for beauty, he realized—the kind of beauty encountered on the streets of Florence, where even manual laborers wore jackets. Clothes didn't have to cost much (all the flaneur's clothes are second hand) but if you put yourself together with personal flair, your individuality and self-expression will brighten Woodstock streets. Surely that was as important as other items on the town's agenda.

It seemed to the flaneur that costume was metaphor, and that in a colony of the arts the most appropriate protest in terms of self-presentation was not grunge, but the beautiful.

It made the world more interesting. How we choose to appear in public is how we show our respect for each other.

It's a beautiful landscape we have starring roles in. We should try to look like we belong here.

Harmonic Convergence

THE FLANEUR LIKES SURPRISES, if they come in the form of kisses. Too often they come in the form of bites to the butt, which keeps him looking over his shoulder. In this story, he gets both.

By nature a contrarian, the flaneur walks facing traffic. He goes against the flow; he stubbornly insists on doing things his way. He doesn't like crowds, so you won't see him where the multitude manifests. He even turned down free tickets and a ride to the Woodstock Festival. Go figure.... Like most born individualists, the flaneur likes to think of himself as extraordinary, but sometimes he suspects he is merely extra-ornery. His dislike of humans in groups is not misanthropic. He likes people—one on one—and he treats them with friendly respect. That is, everyone but hippies; their need to group is alien. He did not like them in the sixties, he does not like them now.

His friends don't understand. They saw hippies as harmless, hirsute wookies, babbling on anachronistically about peace and love, who sometimes showed up with the wide-eyed, reverential look of pilgrims come to drink at the source, asking directions to the Magic Meadow.

In his personal experience, hippies were arrogant, generally and specifically. He was living in Manhattan in the sixties when their tribe invaded his neighborhood. An arrogant hippie chick went topless, riots followed, and the East Village—a rip-off realtor's wet dream—was born. With summers off from good schools, and money from home, hippies sat on the sidewalks begging spare change and mocking him for rushing to work.

He resented their easy assumption of privilege, their playing at Boho life, when their secret, ultimate goal was a cushy top corporate job.

What the flaneur wouldn't cop to was that, down deep, his attitude stemmed from his awareness of class distinctions in America—and in Woodstock. He believed that, like sex, class was omnipresent at every level of society, although seldom acknowledged. The flaneur's background was proudly working class.

Those familiar with hippie history and New Age fads remember the Harmonic Convergence of three decades ago. Summer 1987: allegedly predicted by the Maya, a time when the portents in the heavens converged, and were to open a period of universal peace.

Festivities were held around the country at sacred spots—one of which was Woodstock's Magic Meadow, owned, at the time, by the Woodstock Guild of Craftsmen.

As it happened, the flaneur was the Guild Program Director and one of his duties was to protect the meadow. It was considered a fragile environment, so there were to be no fires and no camping, by anyone, at any time.

In town, the word was out: thousands of New Agers would be camping at the meadow illegally. Apparently the town had no plans to stop them, no desire to, and no means. The flaneur being conscientious, decided that if he couldn't do his job, he could at least go see what was going on. Day was fading on the Green when he started the familiar mountain-climbing trudge up Rock City Road to the meadow. All he could do was pray there were no emergencies. Fire engines would have a hard time getting through. Cars and vans with out of state plates were parked on both sides of the road down to the rec field.

As he expected, most of the cars were new and expensive.

The stream of traffic was continuous. Engines strained, laughter floated from car windows on the night air. Lights came on in the houses he passed. In backyards grill masters were flipping burgers. He was hungry. Seriously ravenous.

To take his mind off his stomach, he tried to imagine the scene he would encounter in the meadow. An orgiastic pagan feast from a Cecil B.DeMille extravaganza came to mind, before he reflected that New Agers were too young to have seen sexy Biblical epics.

He hopped across the brook that gurgles after a heavy rain and stood listening. It was almost quiet. Even the ubiquitous Rainbow tribe drums seemed muted. He had expected to encounter a wall of sound. He mounted the incline that led to the meadow and stood gaping at the encampment that filled his vision. It was neat, orderly: an impromptu tent city, built by people who knew what they were doing. People who respected themselves and their environment. He strolled slowly past campfires from which delicious smells wafted, aware that a wide smile that rose from his long-locked anarchist's heart was taking possession of his face. His world was turned upside down, and something was released in him that felt like freedom.

He recalled something he'd read by Arthur Koestler, something (it had been a long time since he'd read it) about living in a tribe on one side of a mountain, and being scared of the tribe on the other side because they were unknown, and therefore, not human.

Something bit his butt. He looked and saw a child running into the laurel, rubbed the sore spot, laughed, and waited for the kiss.

🔹 🔹 🔹 🔹 🔹

A Day at Mower's Flea Market

🔹 🔹 🔹 🔹 🔹

LIKE MOST MEN, the flaneur dislikes most shopping, largely because it is boring, and perhaps even soul destroying, to spend so much time in malls. Women with money become oniomaniacs, and their husbands, porters. What the flaneur likes is the aleatory messiness of thrift shops, yard sales, and flea markets. In these markets you're likely to be surprised, and to find anything at any price. The flaneur's shopping motto is "Let's keep things the way they used to be," and he has wandered happily through flea markets of New York, Cape Cod, London, Paris, and Tangiers, open to the unexpected, and people-watching as he poked about. Over the years, Mower's has yielded some bargains, the most memorable being a whale's tooth with scrimshaw carving. Browsing the tables at Mower's is like going through Time's attic.

The flaneur often thought it might be fun to sit in a market and watch the world go by, so on a mild Saturday morning mid-August, Will Nixon and the flaneur set up two card tables at the entrance to Mower's field, and laid out copies of their walking book, along with their poetry chapbooks. They were in business. A little later a hot dog vendor parked across the way.

A stone throw's away at Houst's, young men were playing with noisy heavy equipment. The spire of the Woodstock Dutch Reformed Church stabbed the overcast sky above the solar panels on Houst's roof.

When vendors drove onto the field, John Mower guided them to their spots. A former town supervisor, John has the easy, friendly authority of a veteran politician. The Mowers sell their own local histories; the flaneur learned from one that John started the market in 1977, on land purchased by his grandfather in 1907.

Sit in a market for eight hours, and you feel the timelessness of the experience. Markets are as old as history itself. From Babylon onwards, it is capitalism on a human scale. (Flea markets can be traced back to the March aux Puces, in seventeenth-century Paris.)

Some observations about the passing parade: a third of Americans are obese, but it seemed more like half, judging from the unfortunate folks who lumbered by, inexplicably dressed in tight clothing.

Americans dress for comfort, which translates into an aesthetic of ugliness, of which grunge is the extreme. To paraphrase David Sedaris, it's as if they'd been washing shoe polish off a pig, then suddenly threw down the sponge and said, "screw this, I'm going shopping." When the European tourists walked past, they stood out, stylishly put together and slender.

Some people: a woman in a motorized wheelchair rolled past, blessing the flaneur with "peace and love" by waving a sunflower in his direction.

Old friends said hello. Zef and Oona Fessenden stopped to chat; they were herding weekend guests. Zef is a retired attorney, a big man with a big voice who spends most of his time volunteering in Woodstock and Florida. He earned his angel wings long ago.

Judge Frank Engel and his wife came up. Frank and the flaneur reminisced about their friend, assassinologist Rush Harp.

The pace quickened after lunch.

David Segal, brilliant Broadway lighting designer and major Maverick Concerts supporter, said hello. He recently lost his brother Erich, the classicist who wrote *Love Story*.

A handsome blond giant leaned over the table to wish the flaneur well. It was J. J. Blickstein, editor of *Hunger* magazine.

"You can tell the people who don't read," the flaneur said to Will. "They don't even glance our way." Although the two perambulating authors said hello to everyone who passed all day long, two-thirds of market goers did not see them. To non-book lovers they were invisible.

During breaks, the flaneur walked the market, looking for a bargain. He paused before the tarot reader, glanced over the DVDs for sale, checked out the clothes, saw a painting he liked, and came to full flea market alert when he spotted a box full of dirty, mildewed paperbacks. Digging around, he found a first edition of a Charles Willeford novel he could sell for two hundred dollars, and happily paid the vendor his fifty cents. (Over payment, by the way).

He returned to their lemonade stand, exultant about his find.

"It's too bad that people don't realize that our book will be worth more than two hundred dollars one day," Will commented. Then it was time to pack up. The hours had whizzed by.

They had sold a few copies of *Walking Woodstock*, one to a visiting Canadian, who had come for a Levon Helm concert, one to a writer, and one to a major collector and archivist.

Doubtlessly, a twenty-dollar book at a flea market is a hard sell, and they weren't salesmen. Their adventure in bookselling emphasized the value of the middleman—their independently published book was The Golden Notebook's best-selling paperback the previous year.

The flaneur likes the fact that Mower's is an encampment set up in the morning and taken down at night. It's a natural rhythm, and, reminds us that we too set up in our lives and get taken down.

Like a circus, a rock festival, or a traveling theatrical company, a flea market offers a form of entertainment that is transitory. A group of people—the vendors—create a pageant of sorts, offering everything from fresh vegetables to old jewelry, and another group of people—bargain shoppers—come to enjoy the satisfactions of hunting and gathering.

Byrd-ing the Bard
at the Comeau

SUMMER WEEKENDS IN WOODSTOCK bring a parade of tourists to Tinker Street. They start at the Green, take over the sidewalks, and spill over into Tinker Street.

Passing them, the flaneur imagines their disappointment: they don't know what they're looking for, but whatever that is, they did not find it. They came to see Woodstock, and only saw each other, and some T-shirt shops. They turn around before they reach Woodstock Hardware, which is a shame for two reasons: they don't see the Woodstock Library, the town's cultural center; and they miss the Comeau Property, the town's government center as well as its Central Park. And they miss Big Bill.

All they would have to do is to look up at the sign on the side of the hardware store which advertises the Woodstock Shakespeare Festival, with an arrow pointing to Comeau Drive just across the street, to find out one of the town's best kept secrets: people here love the Bard, and attending a performance of "Twelfth Night" is almost as popular as it is in New York's Central Park. It's one of Woodstock's hidden treasures.

But people don't read signs any more.

On a recent Sunday, the flaneur was out for a ramble when he saw the sign, and decided it was time to pay his respects to the Cult of Big Bill, as practiced since 1995 by his friends at Byrd-On-A-Cliff Theatre Company, Elli Michaels and David Aston-Reese. Being himself one of those overeducated Woodstockers with too much time on his hands that he likes to poke fun at, he could afford to take in their latest production of "Twelfth Night."

The great lawn of the Comeau Property was radiant with sunlight almost as thick as syrup. The familiar Elizabethan thrust stage designed by Sal Tagliarino draws the eye but doesn't dominate the open space. A few early birds were spreading blankets for picnics, and even in the distance the flaneur recognized the figure of Freya De Nitto, whom he had once called, in print,"the most beautiful woman in Woodstock." Feminists had frowned, but that first impression, from her days waiting tables at the old Deanie's, had remained with him. Freya might well lay claim to being the last of the Woodstock bohemians. With her husband Ronald, she'd built a house in Byrdcliffe, was partners in a fondly remembered local restaurant, Country Pie, worked as a nude artist's model, chaired the library fair. Hugs and kisses, a glass of wine.

The flaneur asks Ron De Nitto about his painting. Despite his talent and dedication, Ron's art has not yet attracted the attention it richly deserves.

While they caught up, an audience had spread itself around them. Actors appeared on stage. The program announced that this was the Woodstock Shakespeare Festival's nineteenth season. The flaneur had seen every production—dutifully, as an obligation of friendship, because he was weary of Big Bill. He had read and seen the Bard for too long. He agreed with Tolstoy and Shaw, who allowed that Bill was a great poet, but as a playwright, his complicated, corny plots were too much of a muchness. Following the lead of Orson Welles, whose Mercury Theatre production of "Julius Caesar" was in modern dress, this "Twelfth Night" is set in 1920s' Hollywood—and then the anachronistic conceit is promptly forgotten. You settle back to relish the flow of rich language, you wait for the few lines you remember, like the one about cakes and ale, and you realize that you are having a good time. The sun moves its spotlight to the stage. A cool breeze blows. Michael Da Torre was having a fine time channeling Peter Lorre as Malvolio. Bigger than life characters are his meat.

At intermission the flaneur stood to stretch, and look around. The only young people he saw were kids with their parents. It was the same at all the arts venues. Without new blood, arts performers would be left to busk on the street. Were there any modern playwrights the young cared about?

Behind him a group was enjoying a picnic. Prosperous silverbacks. One waved. The flaneur peered at a man who looked vaguely familiar. It was Paul, who owned Catskill Art Supply, disguised by a white beard, with his wife and friends. Long ago he and the flaneur had been kung fu sparring partners. He still had the same joy in his eyes that he'd had back then. It was heartening.

"Twelfth Night" ended. The actors took their bows. As usual, Elli and David, founders and producers of Byrd-On-A-Cliff, had cast themselves. As he shouted his approval, the flaneur thought of the poet W.H. Auden's wonderful line: Let all your thinks be thanks.

If They Catch You,
Eat Your Brains

ONCE UPON A TIME not long ago, as the flaneur likes to say, Woodstock drew movie stars who thought they might want to live here. A local woman recalls leaving Joshua's after lunch when the door opened and a familiar-looking young man held it for her. She looked down—and, shades of Thelma and Louise— saw movie idol Brad Pitt, smiling up at her. She checked to see if he was on his knees, and realized he was seriously short. When she told her friends, she was informed the star was house-hunting in the World's Most Famous Small Town. It seemed appropriate for him to buy here, but he is not on the tax rolls.

The Woodstock Film Festival brings in Hollywood actors, known and unknown, by the bus load, but for the most part, they don't hang out on Tinker Street the way Paul Newman did in the eighties—or like Jane Fonda, when she was filming on Tinker Street a few years back.

Although she was never a star, the flaneur has fond memories of Sylvia Miles, who, in films from *Midnight Cowboy* to *Fare-*

well My Lovely, turned in performances that became indelible in the viewer's memory. The flaneur liked her on the big screen. Her talent helped to redeem a temper that was often on display when she bought the cottage across from the library barn on Library Lane. She put large stones on the street to protect her bushes, and when someone parked, she rushed out, a noisy virago, to defend her stones. She could have collected an Oscar for screeching.

One year the flaneur saw Woodstock native Uma Thurman with her husband Ethan Hawke and their kids at the library fair. He found it difficult to take his eyes from them. It's not often that cinema gods walk among mortals, and the flaneur, a film buff, considered them gods that July day. So did the other fairgoers, who gawked discreetly but did not intrude on their outing.

Viveca Lindfors, a star from an earlier period—call it the Errol Flynn era of costume drama—spent part of a summer in Byrdcliffe producing and starring in a play she presented at the Byrdcliffe Barn. The flaneur went to interview her in her cabin and found to his delight that she was as intelligent and individualistic as her on-screen persona.

One of the flaneur's all-time favorite films is *The Hustler*, in which a young Paul Newman plays an ambitious pool hustler who hooks up with a forlorn Piper Laurie. The flaneur fell for Laurie's Wounded Bird as hard as he did for Lindfors' Queen. He was surprised when long ago he learned that Laurie was a Woodstocker. At a party, he was advised by his hostess to go find Rosie Morganstern. He raised his eyebrows, a feat of heavy lifting he has perfected for social occasions. "Who's she?"

"Piper Laurie."

He went looking for *The Hustler's* tragic figure, but she eluded him. He didn't think of her again until he was ambling past the Village Green and spied the hustler himself, Paul Newman, sitting on a bench quaffing his thirst with a Bud in a wet paper bag. He wondered if Paul and Piper were friends. He imagined what it would be like to see them together on Tinker Street. He wanted more of that dark film.

The flaneur wondered if anyone else shared his wistful notion,that movies continue to unravel in parallel universes. It was at the juncture of dream and reality that he wanted to linger. Standing on the Green, he remembered a mild day in the mid-seventies when he made a full-length feature film on videotape, starting in the spot where he now stood.

It was the year the video revolution hit Woodstock. Everyone wanted to play with the new toy. Parry Teasdale, Ken Marsh, and Gary Hill were the big guns in the new media in town, but erotic writer Marco Vassi and his girlfriend Evelyn Honig had the equipment and wanted to be players as well, so they asked an Off-Broadway actress, who was playing in a revival of *The Three Penny Opera*, if she would appear in a feature to be improvised on Tinker Street.

All they needed was a catchy title and a villain.

That was how *If They Catch You, Eat Your Brains*, came to be made. The first feature made in Woodstock disappeared, as did its star, who was stalked around town by a moper and lurker who signs himself—the Flaneur.

Comic Relief

PEOPLE DON'T MOVE to Woodstock for laughter and parties.

Woodstock is earnest, one might even say heavy. Its Boomer elders carry the weight of the world on their shoulders. The style here is sincere to stodgy; responsibility rules. Flippancy and wisecracking are frowned upon. A long-dead resident dubbed it "the town without foreplay," but that was back when sex was in fashion. Today it might be called "the town without a warm up act—and no laugh track."

A glance through the letters pages of *Woodstock Times* will tell you much of what you need to know about the Most Famous Small Town in the World: there are not a lot of laughs here. The letters are mostly about politics or certified good causes. Their tone is serious, somber, occasionally vicious, often indignant.

We are not happy when we write our screeds to a long suffering WT editor. The flaneur stops reading when the tone gets strident and high minded, and looks around for a cheap laugh.

Aside from the flying visits by professional ticklers, the funniest resident of Woodstock, in the flaneur's admittedly faulty memory, was the Brooklyn-born Irish writer Malachy McCourt, who did a SRO show in Town Hall for the Library Forum series a decade ago.

For a long while, Al Mamlet was the funniest man in the hamlet. Before him, Les Visible challenged political correctness on his cable show. And Ed Sanders' acerbic wit could peel paint. These worthies were quick with one-liners and put-downs, like Sanders' assessment of conservatives as "bitter shitters."

But the flaneur craved silliness. He yearned for the ridiculous, for the wit of Alan Ayckbourn or Charles Ludlam, the sublime door-slamming precision of the great Georges Feydeau. Once you've seen true farce, TV sitcoms are a snooze. But farce is harder to stage than Shakespeare, so the flaneur scrolls Netflix looking for the sons and daughters of Lenny Bruce: stand-up comics who fill theaters by speaking truths we don't want to hear anywhere else—Louis C.K., Doug Stanhope, Bill Burr, Jim Jeffries among others.

Hester Mundis has made the flaneur laugh for over forty years, since she raised an ape named Boris in her Manhattan apartment. She was then an editor and novelist (*Jessica's Wife*), who, upon entering a party, would survey the room and comment, "So this is what I've got to work with." She and her husband Ron Van Warmer—long associated with WDST—lived for many years in a big house in West Shokan. Hester hit her stride when she became the chief writer for the late Joan Rivers, and also warmed up audiences for Joan.

Their approach to humor, from gag writing to delivery, made them a perfect match. Hester seldom appears. To enjoy her, you must know her, or read her books. Unlike many comedians, Hester is "on" almost all the time. Her wit bubbles up from some inexhaustible sources.

Mikhail Horowitz is Court Jester to area culturati and those with I. Q.s above their body temps. When he does his shows at Unison Learning Center and Bearsville Theater with his sidekick Gilles Malkine, he packs them in—and keeps them, pardon the cliché, rolling in the aisles. As often as he can, he brings music into the act, playing a mean flute, with Malkine on guitar, and sometimes a guest.

A flute is the only thing he's mean with. Unlike many comics whose humor is pressed from bile, Horowitz is a mensch – a gentle, well-published poet who has made his own niche in comedy. Many, including the flaneur, have urged him toward television; he would have been a sensation on Letterman, but he demurred. If you want to watch him on screen, get his and Malkine's DVD, "Too Small to Fail." The flaneur is grateful for small silliness, and the way Horowitz keeps his eyeglasses balanced on top of his head like horns during a routine is marvelous.

Bopping with Butterfield at Bearsville

SUMMERS IN THE LATE SEVENTIES when the day's writing had gone well, the flaneur would think of Bearsville, and of sitting at the bar of the Bear Café sipping a martini as the late afternoon sunlight played its dappled magic on the room.

He jumped on his bicycle and headed down the Glenford-Wittenberg Road, past Yankeetown Pond, and then down Wittenberg, to coast into Bearsville, where music impresario Albert Grossman had built an oasis for good food and drink. One Friday afternoon the flaneur had an appointment with a writer, formerly famous, who was living in one of Grossman's properties.

Al Aronowitz was a legend on the music scene for having introduced Dylan to the Beatles. He was music critic for the *New York Post*, and had put together a collection of his best work in a Xerox manuscript he wanted the flaneur to review for *High Times*.

So they sat at the bar and talked, the flaneur paying just enough attention to keep Aronowitz telling stories.

He told them well, and the flaneur was soon caught up in the latest Rolling Stones gossip. The shadows lengthened as he listened to the writer, and he realized it was time to pedal home. They stood up to leave, and at the door bumped into the Baron of Bearsville, the legendary Albert Grossman, a round man whose white hair was tied in a pony tail, accompanied by his friend Barry Feinstein, who sported a luxuriant white mustache that made him resemble a shy walrus.

Outside, Aronowitz told the flaneur that Feinstein was a great photographer of rock stars and film actors. Grossman was Grossman: Dylan's manager. And The Band's. He insisted that the flaneur have a bite and another drink in The Bears, a large house converted into a Chinese restaurant across the way. It was where the musicians hung out when they were recording at Bearsville Studio. The flaneur had met the manager, an American who spoke perfect Mandarin Chinese, and was curious about the place. There had been rumors of parties in the small private rooms upstairs, where coke was laid out on Lazy Susans for the table.

They walked into the bar. It was empty except for a famous face staring out the window. It was Paul Butterfield, the great bluesman (and a Bearsville resident) known as "Butter" to Aronowitz, who introduced the flaneur. Butter was obviously in a serious bad mood.

He glowered at them. The flaneur thought of his bicycle, and wished he'd refused the second martini. Instead, he mentioned Butter's wife Kathy, who had joined a photography cooperative, Cheese, that the flaneur had helped start.

Butter smiled. The ice was broken. The flaneur guessed that the bluesman was nursing a hangover. He listened to the two men talk, and thought about the long ride home. Dusk was blurring the outlines of the trees outside the large bar windows. He had nothing to say to Butterfield, so he kept silent. Then he remembered an article he'd read about Frank Sinatra which had told a disturbing story: leaving a club in Vegas, the singer had spotted a comely young woman he fancied. He sent some persuasive friends to ask her to join him in his suite. Trouble was, she was seated with her husband, and they were newlyweds. He objected to Sinatra's attempt to claim droit du seigneur, and a little later, when he went to the restroom, the persuaders followed and taught him a lesson about celebrity.

The flaneur in those days was fascinated by the idea of celebrity. He told the story, and posed the question: did fame cancel your sense of shame? Aronowitz looked uncomfortable. Nervously, he stuck his finger in his collar to loosen it. Butter glared coldly at the flaneur. "I don't think that happened," he said. "Frank doesn't need to do that. Whoever wrote that garbage is pathetic." The flaneur stood his ground; he knew the author of the piece, Harlan Ellison, and Ellison didn't make things up. Sinatra could sue.

"Look, let me tell you something. I know Frank, and he wouldn't do that. He's always helping people."

The flaneur must have looked skeptical. Butter got angrier, and raised his voice. "I say you writers make this stuff up."

The flaneur decided it was time to leave. Butter looked angry enough to bop him one. The flaneur bade them goodnight. "I'm a friend of Frank's. I know him. You don't," Butter called after him.

It was a long, slow ride home.

Ruckus at Rosa's

THE FLANEUR LIKES HIS STORIES of actors and incidents in our line dance to oblivion to be fair, generous, and true to the last drop; but they must also have bite and heat, or he pushes his plate away. In the case of poetry readings, he is often at a loss for words. As a poet, he is sworn to the way of truth; but the truth about poetry readings is that they are mostly exercises in egotistic futility. How can he say this and keep his poetic license?

He can talk about exceptions. Great readings, or good ones. One exception that came to mind happened on a Sunday afternoon in spring, 1976 at Rosa's Cantina on Rock City Road, across from Woodstock Cemetery. Rosa's was looking to stir up business for its chimichangas, and offered to host readings Sundays, three to five. The flaneur and the Fug agreed to program the series, just as they had agreed to program the Woodstock Library Series upon the death of local poetry doyenne Marguerite Harris.

They imported writers from New York to liven up the home team of Pearl Bond, Marilyn Mohr, Jim Reed, Pat Jackson, Robert DePew Reynolds, etc. Diminutive Spencer Holst came several times to read from his *A Language of Cats*, accompanied by Francine Prose.

But the Fug and the flaneur were not satisfied that they were doing enough in the local poetry scene to honor the memory of their friend Marguerite. To keep themselves amused (poets have a lot of free time, so keeping amused is a priority) they decided to look for the house where Hart Crane had lived when he came to Woodstock for a visit in 1924. And, as the sole acknowledged great poet to have spent more than a weekend here, they decided to honor him with a reading of his masterpiece, *The Bridge*. Rosa's would host a poetry event so high of brow that they could look down on the Academy of American Poets that Sunday, June 1st. They assembled a cast of readers: Marilyn Allen, Mark Zuss, Bob Paton, and the sole professional actor, John LeFever, and met for rehearsals.

The Fug and the flaneur never found the Crane house, but the reading of *The Bridge* was a great success. An audience of fifty packed the cantina. Among them sat Phillip Guston, one of the great American painters, chain-smoking Camels. It seemed that everyone understood what they were watching.

As he listened to the voices of the other readers, the flaneur recalled his first summer in New York, when he and his friends would rise before dawn and walk across the Brooklyn Bridge reciting Crane's magnificent visionary lines: "How many dawns, chill from his rippling rest / the seagull's wings shall dip and pivot him..." They had never failed to make the fine hairs on the back of his neck stand up. He thought the other readers were exceeding their normal abilities, transcending ego and even personality to become one with the muse and raise the bones of the drowned poet from the "cruel bottom" of the sea. He looked out the window and watched a turkey buzzard circle over the cemetery across the street. After giving over fifty readings himself, he wanted to return to the quiet communion with words on a page—the right words in the right, inevitable order. He wanted to be the watcher, not the watched.

In order to draw an audience for featured readers, poetry venues often tack on an "Open Mic" slot so that amateur Percy Dovetonsils can have a brief moment in the spotlight. Afterward venues expect MCs to clear the place for paying customers. But some readers won't relinquish the mic. Such a reader was Robert DePew Reynolds, who was notable for his execrable verse, a ready smile, dreadlocks, and a rowdy following. He looked the part of the beat poet, and since he was drunk, acted it. He had taken up twice his allotted time, and the bartender was signaling the flaneur that his time was up. The flaneur cut the mic, and announced to Bob's claque, none of whom had heard *The Bridge*, that the reading would continue across the street in the cemetery. There Bob mounted a tomb and continued his rant. Not long after, he was walking in the dark and struck by a car. He never recovered. After his funeral in the Dutch Reformed Church, his friends followed him to the scene of his triumph, the Woodstock Cemetery.

Casualties of the Arts

IN THE COLONY OF THE ARTS there is a tendency to make romantic figures of artists whose lives here have been filled with privation and suffering. Testimonials and histories omit the human cost of art. The sad story of the artist John G. Ernst, his poet wife Pearl Bond, and their doomed daughter Della might interest parents who are fearful that their children will chose art classes over law school, bohemian sacrifice over bourgeois comforts.

The flaneur first encountered John Ernst on the Village Green one summer afternoon. Even for casual Woodstock, his attire was comfortable...even louche, consisting of satin boxing trunks and nothing else. (John was a small man, a flyweight, and no pugilist.)

He was enjoying beer in a paper bag, and appeared to be waiting for the noon Trailways bus. At his feet, on a baby blanket, were spread watercolor landscapes. He sucked on his beer with a toothless mouth. His sunken cheeks and round, haunted eyes were suitable for a story by Poe. Even sitting at a bus stop in bright sunlight, he was surrounded by an invisible cloak of melancholy.

When the bus pulled up, he went into action. From somewhere he produced an artist's beret, carefully placing it on his head like a crown, with the same sad dignity Chaplin summoned for his Little Tramp.

The flaneur was transfixed– especially so when he saw tears glistening in the little artist's great Keane eyes. His approach was soft sell, his prices rock bottom. Needless to say, he sold out. The flaneur bought two landscapes, the first of what would become a large collection of John's primitive dashed-off, beer-money sketches.

The next time the flaneur saw John Ernst was at a poetry reading at the Woodstock Public Library run by a grandmotherly television actress named Marguerite Harris. The evening's fare was poetry by Pearl Bond, whose small talent had gotten her into the pages of *Poetry* magazine. She looked—and indeed, turned out to be—an unhappy poeticule of the party of resentment, the kind of woman for whom complaint is as natural as breathing. But sitting next to her was the sad-sack flyweight from the Green, regarding her with pride and bitterness. The look was not loving. Perhaps she had reason to complain, the flaneur thought. After the reading, the flaneur helped Marguerite stack and put away chairs, and she filled him in on John and Pearl.

"John, it is said, was a trapeze artist for Ringling Bros. and Barnum & Bailey Circus before World War Two." Here Marguerite paused to give a slow theatrical wink in which her eyelashes became whiplashes. "It is even said that he was Burt Lancaster's partner on the high wire, although there's not a scrap of evidence. What we know is obvious: he's a souse who can get mean. Pearl bruises easily...."

Pearl Bond was a woman of heft. She made two of her flyweight husband. If she sat on him, her avoirdupois would surely crush him. Marguerite continued building her case against Ernst as an imp of evil, but the flaneur had a final question: what made the imp so sad?

"He never recovered from the war. He was assigned to graves detail. He was up to his ass in death for days without relief."

The flaneur sighed, imagining John surrounded by piles of corpses. No wonder he looked haunted.

In those days—the mid-eighties—the flaneur still occasionally found himself at the wheel of some Detroit behemoth, and would pick up John, who often hitched into town for a tall cold one. Usually he ended up buying a watercolor. John would talk about Pearl's poetic effusions, or his woebegone daughter, Della, but never about himself. The phenomenon of post-traumatic stress was recognized among Vietnam vets, but John never spoke of his grave duties. The flaneur, remembering Al Capp's Li'l Abner comic strip, thought of John as the Capp character Joe Btfsplk, who walked around with a black cloud over his head.

Once, the flaneur encountered John selling his wares on the steps of the Woodstock Guild of Craftsmen on Tinker Street. John said Pearl had kicked him out, and he was living in the crawl space under the Guild porch. He added, shaking his head and looking up at the sky like a modern Job, that his daughter had killed herself. The tears fell. He sipped his beer.

John died in 1995 at the age of seventy-five. Pearl predeceased him by six years. There have been shows of John's work. He seems to have a modest but stable reputation.

The Artists' Cooperative

EXPERIMENTS IN COOPERATIVE LIVING and working flourished in the sixties. When the flaneur arrived in New York in 1962, he lived in a crash-pad cooperative for the summer. When he moved to Woodstock in 1972, he encountered the Carey Family, whose family commune, the True Light Beavers, was Woodstock's most successful experiment in coop living. When the flaneur decided he wanted to start an art gallery, it was the communal model he chose.

With a partner, the painter Paul Naylor, he looked for a gallery space, and found one quickly: a barn at the promisingly named Parnassus Square, on the corner of Lower Byrdcliffe and Rock City Roads. Across the road at Folk Art, a parrot greeted customers. A block away, the flaneur rented a house for his family on Simmons Drive, next door to a house with a teepee where pianist Warren Bernhardt lived with his lovely wife Jan. During May 1973 Paul and the flaneur made the huge barn into a gallery space and interviewed prospective coop members. Barbara Neustadt, Gary Hill, Paul Tucker, Tom Miner, Howie Greenberg, Dan McCormack, and Alan Carey became the core group. They were eager to show their work, but getting them to do more mundane tasks, like gallery sitting, or cleaning up, was like herding cats. Many a sixties commune broke up on the rocks of housework. The flaneur did not repine. He had dreamed of his own gallery, and he wanted to see up close how anarchy worked. He was happy that others shared his curiosity.

As is usual in such situations, he who does the lion's share of the work is first among equals. The flaneur wrote press releases and took out the garbage. When people didn't come to openings, he got the word out so that they were afraid they'd miss, for instance, his poet friend Daniella Gioseffi seducing an audience to listen to her read with her steamy belly dancing. Over a hundred art lovers appeared, and continued to come to the barn to concerts, art openings, film and video showings, and readings (by Gary Burr, Jack Fenton, Malcolm Braly, and a dozen more) that the flaneur arranged from 1973 to 1974.

By July of its first summer, The Artists' Coop was a Saturday afternoon destination, and many artists had a designated-driver good time. It might have been called the Carlo Rossi Circuit, for the maker of the jug wine that made the art talk flow. Art mavens would attend a decorous opening at The Gallery of July and August, to see the work of Ancil Chasteen and Jolyon Hofsted, then hit the WAAM to see what the older generation was up to. (Not much, in the flaneur's opinion.)

Unexpectedly, for there was little money for ads, the coop became popular. The older painters came to scoff, and stayed to toot their own horns. The young coop artists listened politely, and thereafter ignored the art colony's fine landscape artists. Fresh talent made Parnassus Square jump. They talked of video, which was then establishing itself as a new art form. Gary Hill used the coop to place himself at the center of the video revolution. From California, Gary was a surfer and champion skateboarder. (Today he calls Seattle home, and he works in Intermedia.) Howie Greenberg, like Alan Carey, was a photographer for the *Woodstock Times*. Today he owns the premiere photo gallery in New York, and represents the estates of many famous photographers.

A coop opening brought out a crowd that overflowed the small white gravel parking area in front of the old barn. At one opening the flaneur spotted a deeply tanned, handsome, sixtyish man who stood out like a peacock among chickens. He seemed to be lecturing, if not chastising, a friend of the flaneur's. Irwin Touster headed the art department at Parsons School of Design, and, as art critic for the *Woodstock Times*, was probably the most hated man in Woodstock. His motto seemed to be, if the truth hurts, why lie? He had spoken of the peacock, William Pachner, as if he was the sole authentic artist in a town where they hid up every tree. Standing with the two men, the flaneur could sense the frustration bubbling up like hot grease in Irwin's psyche. He lived to issue opinions and to win arguments, but he did not dare interrupt Pachner's diatribe about Woodstock artists. The flaneur heard his own thoughts about the Woodstock art scene expressed in impeccable English, with a Viennese flavoring. They agreed that the best painters were Phil Guston and Bud Plate (whose death at forty-five was recent). The flaneur brought up cooperative working and living, and Pachner predicted (correctly) that the coop would fold once the flaneur dropped it. Irwin left them, and gradually everyone did. They talked on, standing alone in the parking lot, both aware that they had embarked on a lifelong friendship.

Gallery Cruising

I

SINCE HIS SELF-APPOINTED TASK IS TO SEE, and to remember, the flaneur longs to truly see what he's looking at, the way that he imagines artists do, when they are good – or lucky. He remembers that he really saw a tree as if for the first time in a Chinese ink brush drawing class. Wielding the brush opened his inner eye.

To look. To see. He should be able to. After all, he's spent a lifetime looking at art. His first wife was a painter. He founded and directed a legendary Woodstock art gallery, and edited a county arts magazine. He's hung out with artists all his life.

But if he cannot put what he sees into words, the flaneur is functionally blind. Still, he knows what he likes—and recently in Woodstock he's looked at a lot of art. He has decided to visit every gallery in town to assess the state of the arts in the Colony of the Arts.

His method would be simple: try to attend openings whenever possible, because that's where you can overhear talk about art, and get some idea of the excitement being caused by it, then return on a quiet day to look at what was on the walls. He had no wish to be critical, or even informative. He would see what he would see, and record his impressions, and some memories.

He remembered that on summer weekends in the seventies, there might often be three or four openings where the conversation flowed as fast as the cheap California jug wine was poured. It was easy to move from one gallery to the next, getting progressively more sloshed and excited about art. The point was not primarily to sell, but to share your work and show it off. Since this was before computers, people talked about art and not tech-dreck.

The Center for Photography at Woodstock

THE FIRST THING the flaneur noticed when he attended the Center for Photography at Woodstock's "Surface Tension" opening of the work of eleven photographers was a lack of excitement. Three dozen people milled about, mouse quiet, all in their twenties and thirties. The second thing he noticed was that there was no wine. This was a serious MFA-type crowd. The mostly abstract daubs on the walls demonstrated how far the art of photography had become unmoored from its beginnings in realism. One exhibitor, Matthew Brandt, had made a cautious nod to the elderly avant-garde with portraits of people, "salted paper prints," personalized with the bodily fluids of his subjects. Cost of each: four thousand dollars. (Unframed.)

Feeling fogey-ish, the flaneur made his way outside into the sunlight. He stood for a moment blinking on the empty porch, wishing it was still the Café Espresso, and he could sit and think about what he'd seen over a cold brew. He remembered the Center's very first exhibition—a group show of one hundred photos entitled "Why Photography" in May 1977, when the gallery was on the second floor. What came to mind was Baudelaire's first reaction in 1850 to the new art: that it was a morbid narcissistic disease, "mere technology." (Of course, he then sat for the great pioneering photographer Nadar a number of times.)

The flaneur remembered Cheese, the photo cooperative that preceded the opening of the Center. Howie Greenberg was a member, along with Paul Butterfield's wife Kathy. Howie was a founder of The Center for Photography, and is now perhaps the most important photography dealer in New York.

The flaneur concluded that perhaps Baudelaire had been right. From Walker Evans to Robert Mapplethorpe, photographers had been of more interest to the flaneur than most of what happened in the art world, but now, in trying to be painterly, photography had become mere technology.

Kleinert-James Gallery

TO ENTER THE Kleinert-James Gallery you must pass through a crafts shop that sells ersatz Byrdcliffe crafts, and mount a few steps. The flaneur pauses at the entrance, feeling like one who has returned home after a long absence to find that strangers have moved in and changed all the furniture around. He feels slightly disoriented. For twelve years in the eighties and nineties he had served as the Woodstock Guild's Program Director, and had attended every opening in that small space. He had introduced hundreds of performers on that stage. It was his living room.

The show on the walls was called "Micromorphic" and it consisted of thirty-seven abstract representations of tiny rocks that looked like bubbles. Sometimes it is possible to stand in one spot, glance around, and see all that you want to see. He did so, respectfully, and closed his eyes.

Twenty years before in this space, performance artist Carolee Schneemann had caused a sensation by pulling a scroll from her vagina. There had been plenty of conventional shows of paint on canvas, but memory of them had dimmed. He was pleased to think that Carolee's work—she showed at Bard—still drew crowds. MIT Press had published a fat book about her work.

The dark space depressed him. He was glad to step outside into the bright May sunlight. Before going to the opening of the Woodstock Artists Association and Museum's regional members' show, he would sit once more on the porch of the Guild in the "Poet's Corner," and watch the tourist parade down Tinker street.

He gave little thought to the Guild these days.

WAAM

THE FLANEUR APPROACHED the members show with some trepidation. There had been so many mediocre shows over the years that he had stopped going. Then there had been the wars within the organization. (Artists know how to slip a handmade shiv under the ribs.) Even his friend Aileen Cramer, a volunteer and a doyenne of the old guard, had been wounded.

So, expecting the worst, he was happily surprised to find the gallery crowded with excited people talking about art. The show was nothing less than superb. Maybe the lithic bubbles from the Kleinert show had gone to his head, but he found three works that made him see. The first was a landscape worthy of being placed next to anyone in the Hudson River School: a landscape by Jane Bloodgood-Abrams titled "Nocturne" which had won the Kate Mariel Diana Award. He stood before it to see what truly good painting was. Then across the room he looked at Lowell Miller's "Neck Support," a small jewel-like bronze of a neck in a brace. It gleamed with unholy light, as if forged by a demonic dwarf in the Devil's blacksmith shop. Truly beautiful. Another award-winning piece, "Front Porch" by Scott Gill, was a timeless double portrait on scratchboard that stays in his memory. The Towbin Wing in the rear offered a chance to see work by George Ault. The flaneur left WAAM encouraged about art in Woodstock.

II

FOR A SMALL WORLD, art carries vast museums full of meaning. The flaneur thinks of it mostly as an artist's response to the world, as in these lines from William Bronk: "The arts having something to tell us/ It is not what we wanted to hear;/ but we listen./ It is a very private communication./ It becomes our life."

Art may also be a poignant mirror of its time, materially and spiritually. Decades hence, when people think of the sixties, they will think of Andy Warhol's soup cans. And what images will they have of today's Woodstock?

The Fletcher Gallery

THE FLETCHER GALLERY, on Mill Hill Road, specializes in the work of dead Woodstock artists. The day the flaneur climbed its stairs a voice from above, as if from the heavenly precincts, greeted him. A woman sat at a desk working. Paintings crowded the wall, floor to ceiling, the way they would have in a nineteenth-century Paris salon, all the familiar names, some of them people he had known, like John Ernst, some of the artists, still living. The work was good—competently executed. Safe investments for collectors. They were responses to the life of their time, but as he admired them, the flaneur was saddened: These works were as dead as their makers. It wasn't their age, or the periods mirrored, it was their blindness, he thought, surprised. These artists had worked assiduously, but without vision.

Galerie BMG

GALERIE BMG perches on the high bank of the Tannery Brook opposite the exit from Houst's alcove, with a bigger room upstairs specializing in contemporary photography.

The flaneur was still puzzling over his reaction to the work he had seen in the Fletcher Gallery, so at first he gazed blankly—yes, unseeing—at the principal show by Bryan David Griffith, titled collectively "In a Big World Wandering."

He knew the art at Fletcher did not seem dead because it was "dated." All art was of its time. Perhaps it was because it lacked singularity?

He turned his attention to Bryan Griffith's work. Soft focus, surreal, a trifle sentimental—little figures lost in a big world.

Then he saw it: One of the figures was crossing a bridge. He stared. He saw, because the artist had seen. He knew the image would stay with him all his life. He would return to Galerie BMG.

The Elena Zang Gallery

AFTER DAYS OF dour spring rain, the moody sun cracked a smile over Lake Hill just as Mary Frank arrived at the Elena Zang Gallery to attend the opening party for her new work. A national figure, Frank lives in Bearsville, and has made friends and admirers in the area. The flaneur anticipated a crowd. He walked into the small sunlit gallery with expectations that were immediately met. On one wall were a series of silhouettes of female figures that might have been drawn in the Lascaux caves by Leonardo da Vinci—had he been a woman. The energy shown in the simple lines was the result of Frank's artistry—and her ability to see the eternal. He was greeted warmly by Elena, who pointed out that she was wearing shoes in honor of the occasion. The flaneur thought he could still be bought with a kiss.

He stepped outside onto the lawn, and headed to the refreshment table for a glass of white wine poured by Lucinda Knaus. A broad lawn sloped down to a babbling brook crossed by a small bridge. Steps led up to a meadow where outdoor sculpture could be admired. The flaneur never gazed upon this bucolic scene without thinking of Coleridge's lines: "In Xanadu did Kubla Khan/ A stately pleasure dome decree..."

The purpose of an opening party is to draw attention to the work by offering art mavens an opportunity to mingle for a good cause. The A-list of Woodstock culturati showed up for Mary Frank. The flaneur said hello to the novelist James Lasdun, Terry

Funk-Antman, a therapist specializing in meditation, and artist Stella Chasteen. The crowd was mostly older, but one young woman with green hair showed up. Cleo, the resident puppy, patrolled the ground looking for crumbs.

The Varga Gallery

THE VARGA GALLERY, on Tinker Street next to the movie house, is hard to miss. Just look for tall daisies in an overgrown front yard that any other town would have cited as an eyesore. It's not, of course. The flaneur found it refreshing. But he had to admit, the Varga gallery was the personification of funk and punk. In her years running the gallery (and hoping that her dreamboat David Bowie would stop in on the way to his nearby home) Varga had made her gallery a haven for outsider and visionary art. Now for the first time, she was having a solo show of her own work. The flaneur entered the small, dark space and found Christina Varga being videotaped by videographer Dave Menzies. Christina greeted him warmly. It had been a day for kisses. Squeezing through the crowd, the flaneur looked at the Varga oeuvre: large canvases on which collages of big breasted women cut from pinup magazines drew at least the male gaze. He couldn't tell whether the artist was making a pro- or anti-sex statement, so he walked outside where aging hippies were loudly lamenting the good old days of raucous poetry reading at the Three Penny Café, long gone now. He thought back to the seventies, when the Varga had been the Gallery of July and August, showing work by Ancil Chasteen and William Pachner. No daisies then....

The flaneur sighed, thinking about the thousands of openings he had gone to. What a peculiar ritual it was, but on a spring day what fun!

III

THE FLANEUR and his Beautiful Wife were staying, courtesy of a friend, in a prewar building on West Tenth Street in the heart of Greenwich Village in late summer. They had decided to visit new museums or ones they hadn't seen in years. For the flaneur, it was like coming home. He had lived a few blocks east for a decade when he was young, and of course he wanted to show his BW the old neighborhood.

The experience was like stepping into a time machine. Crossing Third Avenue at Cooper Union, they walked, bobbing and weaving, through crowds of young people in punk loungewear, down St. Marks Place. He pointed out where the Dom had been—"We'd all go dancing there until the Warhol crowd took it over." Across the street, the Five Spot had offered the best jazz in the city. "We would get there early to claim a table when Thelonius Monk was scheduled." At the end of the block, the flaneur pointed out the building where W.H. Auden had lived in princely squalor. The poet was sometimes encountered on the block shuffling along in carpet slippers, his fissured turtle face wreathed in cigarette smoke.

At the corner of Second Avenue the flaneur thought he had fallen down a rabbit hole. A dozen neo-hippies sat in powwow on the sidewalk. It was suddenly 1968, he was walking home from work, and the future awaited. Here was that future he had looked forward to: youth imitating the sixties, but without the idealism or prosperity of that irretrievable wonderful/awful time.

Manhattan is a constant assault on the eyes. There is simply so much to take in that you can't see the trees for the forest. Every instant your vision is bombarded with thousands of impressions, of which you may apprehend a dozen.

As he walked the molten Manhattan streets observing the superimposition of the new upon the old and dodging ghosts, the flaneur repeated a mantra he had developed leading tours of Tinker Street: "Look down, look up." Mountains are one key to Woodstock's development. Bluestone for sidewalks is another. When you look up in Manhattan, all you see are the towers where the Masters of the Universe lurk. But if you look down, quite often you'll find that you're standing on Woodstock bluestone.

The National Academy Museum on Museum Mile above the Metropolitan showcases the kind of social realism that dominated art in Woodstock for over four decades. As far as the flaneur was concerned, the painters on exhibit had not truly seen what was before them the way documentary photographers had.

Discouraged, he followed his BW to the next stop: the Jewish Museum, and the work of Edouard Vuillard (1868-1940). The flaneur walked slowly through the exhibit, studying Vuillard's portraits of the bourgeoisie. Much of the work was dark in tone and not quite finished. He thought of Proust: these were his people sitting for their portraits. The painter's artistry had granted them immortality because he had seen them more deeply than any photographer could.

They went to the Metropolitan for lunch in the cafeteria and then made their way to the American Wing. The flaneur wanted to see the work of the Hudson River school. Something Will Nixon said had intrigued him. In the twenties and thirties, Woodstock artists were top dogs, and the work of the nineteenth-century landscape artists was relegated to dusty antique shops. But today the paintings of Thomas Cole—who took a wagon to the top of Overlook in August 1846—have pride of place, and Woodstock artists are nowhere to be seen. As he cruised the galleries of the museum, the flaneur reflected on the vagaries of artistic fashion: Was it any wonder that even successful artists he knew often had a haunted, half-crazed look? On top one minute, on the bottom the next....

There was one other place the flaneur wanted to show his BW.

An electrified gas lamp—the only one remaining of the thousands that once illuminated Manhattan—stands lonely vigil at the entrance to Patchin Place, a nineteenth- century courtyard just a few steps from Sixth Avenue, across from Jefferson Market Library in the Village. Every time he came to New York the flaneur came here to stand under the lamp and conjure up the ghosts of the great literary figures who had lived here: Theodore Dreiser, e.e. cummings, and Djuna Barnes.

It was Barnes, the author of the modern classic *Nightwood*, who had inspired the flaneur and a friend to pay their respects with a bouquet of flowers.

The flaneur stood looking up at who he was in August 1962, thinking of how this little enclave of silence in the thunderous city had become a portal into the past.

The BW wanted to see the new Rubin Museum of Art at 150 West Seventeenth Street. The flaneur was happy to walk Seventeenth Street because it brought back memories of Manhattan in the early seventies when he was managing editor of a national magazine that was both hip and louche, with offices not far from the museum.

Located in a former Barneys, the Rubin is the premiere museum for the display of Himalayan art in the West. It gleams with money and style—the graphic part of it supplied by Woodstocker Milton Glazer. On the second floor figurines centuries old are displayed like jewels at Tiffany's. The displays invited an aesthetic response without a spiritual context, although there is a prayer room with blazing candles and incense not far away. The flaneur was reminded of the giant gold Buddha at KTD on Overlook Mountain.

As he stared at the unfamiliar iconography, the flaneur fell into a light trance. It was a meditative state he recognized. If you look long enough at things without naming them, they reveal themselves to you.

It was in this state that the flaneur went to use the facilities. He locked the door and gasped. It was the best-designed restroom he'd ever seen. Standing washing his hands, it came to him: Beauty is truly in the eye of the beholder. It was wherever you could see it. It did not need to be painted, drawn, or framed. He laughed at the comedy of finding beauty—and a way of seeing—in a museum pissoir, and the platitude that had come to mind. Nevertheless he winked at the blind fool in the mirror with gratitude: Take your lessons where you find them. Keep looking and you will see.

Woodstock Poetry Festival

ALTHOUGH IT WAS COVERED EXTENSIVELY by the media, if you google Woodstock Poetry Festival you will search in vain for memories of the historic event held here at the turn of this century, which were the only readings the flaneur has seen that deserved the "festival" appellation. You will find references to the WPF of Oxford, England where the flaneur did a reading long ago; and to the WPF hosted at Woodstock Library in the seventies by Marguerite Harris, later by the flaneur and the Fug, and more recently by Phillip Levine. A confusion of festivals?

Implicit in the word "festival" is celebration and the promise of merriment—good food, good drink, and perhaps even a roll in the hay. Put "poetry" next to it, and forget conviviality, you've got a linguistic con, like "industrial park" and "corporate campus." But the three summer poetry festivals assembled by Laurie Ylvisaker with the assistance of the flaneur and a committee of a dozen that included Gioia Timpanelli, BobWright, Tom Fletcher, Larry Berke, Barry Samuels, Saul Bennett, Tad Richards, Susan Sindall, Nancy Butler and many others, were glamorous, exciting, world-class affairs.

It was obvious on the first morning of the festival that it would be a success. The principal venue, where the visiting poets would read, was the Bearsville Theater. Its lobby was crowded with ticket holders. They came out for featured readers: Poet Laureate Billy Collins; Robert Creeley; Stephen Dunn, that year's Pulitzer Prize winner; and Sharon Olds; backing up these stars were dozens of local readers. Putting this town- wide event together was a labor of love for Laurie Ylvisaker and the flaneur. They worked well together, bringing, in 2002, Lawrence Ferlinghetti, Michael McClure, Sharon Olds,and Li-Young Lee; and in 2003, John Ashbery, Paul Muldoon, and Naomi Shihab Nye.

The flaneur, despite years of experience as a Program Director, was astonished by the number and volubility of the poetry lovers brightly chattering around him. Where had they been hiding? He fantasized an underground cell of poetry lovers holding secret meetings by moonlight at which they recited not Ginsberg, but John Keats.

(The closest reality came to this fantasy happened one afternoon when the flaneur, on a break, was sitting in a sylvan glade in the little park where Albert Grossman lies buried. He was riffing with his friend Mikhail Horowitz that he was probably scouting talent among the moles and voles. Then Mikhail cupped his ear, and whispered theatrically, "Hark! It is our poet laureate pitching woo." The flaneur heard Billy Collins reciting one of his poems to a giggling fan, followed by the unmistakable sounds of passionate smooching.)

Laurie, who brought legendary names in American poetry to the Bearsville Theater, Byrdcliffe Theater, the Fletcher Gallery and the Woodstock Library, came from Woodstock aristocracy. Her grandfather, Henry Morton Robinson, was the author of *The Cardinal*, a perennial bestseller and classic Otto Preminger film.

She grew up in Woodstock, attended SUNY New Paltz, and made it big in Florida real estate. She spent freely to ensure the success of the festival: fees, airfares, cars and drivers. Today she is a successful Woodstock realtor.

Looking back on the experience of helping to run a large festival, the flaneur surprises himself when he realizes that what he enjoyed most was not the planning, but dealing with the emergencies that came up.

The flaneur felt energized by his discovery of a new talent. While he had long before decided that if a thing is worth doing, it is worth doing badly, he was gratified to think that sometimes what he did saved the day. When one of the festival's featured guests, the Arab American poet Naomi Shihab Nye, was about to go on, it was discovered that there was no one to introduce her; the flaneur stepped in—awkwardly, perhaps, but he got the job done.

One night he wasn't so lucky. The Maverick Concert Hall, a venue where both featured poets and locals were to read, was packed with fans who had come to hear Robert Creeley and Galway Kinnell. There was a break, and a talented college student was introduced.

She began, but nothing came through the mic. Despite the flaneur's signals, she refused to stop. Despite angry clapping, she refused to look up from her manuscript. She was frozen, her bird-like voice barely audible. The flaneur felt terrible for her. Then he had an idea. The girl's father was in the dressing room. He was a congressman, a rock- and-roll star; surely she would listen to such a father.... But her father refused. "She should have checked her equipment," he said.

It would be years before the flaneur realized that the young poet's father had been right. His help would have upstaged her.

"Everybody Knows, Everybody Goes"

LIKE THE REST OF HUMANITY, most writers soon vanish from collective memory once they answer the Reaper's knock. Woodstock is filled with the ghosts of estimable writers worth a glance back from those on the moving sidewalk of life. If they achieved sufficient recognition while alive, if they won prizes or celebrity, they are more likely to cast a long shadow over those who are yet vertical. But competition is stiff, and eventual oblivion certain. As good Dr. Browne in *Urn Burial* says, "In vain do individuals hope for immortality, or any patent from oblivion." Here are a few names to look back at.

When the flaneur moved to Woodstock, he took an apartment in a house on Calamar Lane not far from the cinema. His neighbors, Eli and Marie Waldron, were Greenwich Villagers related to the flaneur's friend Rush Harp. Marie had the long-suffering look the wives of alcoholics get. Eli was a writer with a big-city rep, but since he was taking Antabuse rather than martinis, he was taciturn. It was only after his death in 1980 that we learned what a talent was lost.

Eli published stories, magazine pieces, and poems in *The Saturday Evening Post* and *The New Yorker*. He was friends with J.D. Salinger and Herman Wouk. In a memorial tribute, legendary *New Yorker* editor William Shawn spoke glowingly of his great promise. Perhaps booze derailed the progress of his career, but it didn't kill him. He died in a car crash. When the flaneur knew him, he was a defeated-looking man with a quiet, dry wit—as exemplified by this line from his grave marker: "Everybody knows, Everybody goes."

Every literate Woodstocker knows that Hart Crane, a major American poet, lived here for a brief time in the mid-twenties. Overlooked is an English poet with a much bigger reputation back then. Richard Le Gallienne was one of the Yellow Book set of the eighteen-nineties. He had known Yeats, Swinburne, and Oscar Wilde. Unlike Crane Le Gallienne was active in the village. He wrote a history of Woodstock.

The great British novelist John Cowper Powys lived across the river, and he would come over to hike the Catskills with Le Gallienne, whom he described as looking every inch the handsome poet.

As a teenager in darkest Ohio, the flaneur first read *The Brothers Karamazov*, edited by a Woodstocker named Manuel Komroff (1890-1974). He was a screenwriter, playwright, and a novelist, probably best known for writing *The Scarlet Empress*, a classic Marlene Dietrich vehicle.

He ended his days in Bearsville, as did Edmund Gilligan (1890-1973) a novelist whose principal subject was the sea.

Depression and despair are concomitant with the writer's trade. Seeking fame is like musical chairs. Two of the flaneur's friends adjusted rope neckties, and stepped into eternity. Since anger is said to motivate many suicides, the flaneur can imagine their last thoughts: This will show them; maybe now they will acknowledge my genius. Of course, no one paid attention.... Wives remarried, kids hated them. As for the general public—out of sight, out of mind. Suicide is not a good career move, despite the fatal hijinks of Berryman, Plath, and Sexton.

And should you grab the brass ring, as Maverick novelist Henry Morton Robinson did with *The Cardinal*, which became a Hollywood classic, what then? The movie is still screened, but the novel has been pulped to make more beach reads. His contemporary, Ira Wolfert, faced the same end.

Writers are often remembered not because they wrote well, or their books sold well, but because they somehow come to exemplify their times. Think of hippies in the sixties, and you think of Abbie Hoffman. Think of sexuality then, and the flaneur's guess is that one day a Woodstocker named Marco Vassi will come to mind. Vassi wrote one of the essential books of the sixties, *The Stoned Apocalypse*, an account of his adventures with the fads of that decade. He also wrote a slew of erotic novels which caused *The New York Times* chief book critic to hail him as America's best erotic writer. (He wasn't, but no matter.) Saul Bellow seconded the nomination.

Marco's residence here was off and on from the sixties to the eighties. He wrote a column for the *Woodstock Times*, upsetting people who in person found him charming. The ladies loved him. But he had the fatal need for fame—to be a guru, actually—an incarnation of the Maitreya Buddha.

He died of complications from AIDS in 1983, the result of having unprotected sex with infected partners. Depressed, he committed suicide by HIV.

The flaneur will not forget him.

"Cut is the branch that might have grown full straight, / And burned is Apollo's laurel bough." – Christopher Marlowe.

La Vida es Dura:
Janine Pommy Vega

A SPRING NIGHT on Route 212. The two poets had given a reading in Kingston at the Sturgeon Wine Bar on the Rondout. Now they were returning home to Woodstock, tired but happy, to sleep in separate beds with new lovers. They were still young, and everything that happened still meant something. The SRO audience had been enthusiastic, and the basket on the back seat was stuffed with bills, even some twenties. They were juiced, but could still walk a straight line.

The flaneur, riding shotgun, saw them first. The dark road was carpeted with tiny creatures hopping blindly where biology drove them. There were too many to count—a sight to make a blind man see double. Hundreds of baby frogs crossing the road, many flattened by their tires. Janine Pommy Vega stood on the brakes. "Hoppy frogs!" she cried, leaping from the car and kneeling to inspect the damage she had inflicted on the tiny amphibian army. Janine mourned them the way she had performed—as if she'd known everyone in the audience and been intimate with more than a few—all her life. It was as if she thought she could inflate the flattened ones by incantation. Cars were stopping behind them. Janine dabbed her eyes and they pulled away from the scene of the crime. "Life is hard for small things," she said. "La vida es dura."

Janine was fearless. She gave you the impression that she had done and seen enough for two lifetimes, that she was unstoppable. After all, right after high school she moved in with the Ginsberg crowd, and became tight with ur-Beat Herbert Huncke. She married young, traveled the world and slogged through her personal slough of despond of drugs and prostitution. The flaneur met her when she wandered into his East Village bookstore in the sixties, and they became friends in the Woodstock of the seventies.

Janine was one of the few Beat women writers to achieve international fame as a poet. She was always being invited on reading tours in Yugoslavia or California, and she worked as a poet in the schools and prisons to make ends meet, travel, and maintain her base in Willow.

Her public readings were local events, usually sold out. She brought a preacher's fire and passion to these performances that thrilled audiences, she lived every day with the same energy.

She poured her passionate nature into everything she did—poetry, politics, travel, teaching, and hiking. The few times the flaneur went for a walk with her she had to scramble to keep up. In the end, her feet did her in—arthritis and surgeries to keep her mobile sapped her strength—but her courage never failed.

The Curse of the Mohicans

THERE IS A CURSE on Woodstock that periodically drives ordinary decent people to do battle against their neighbors with a rage disproportionate to whatever issue is in dispute.

When the flaneur first heard of this curse he scoffed. Native Americans would hunt here, but would not live here. Why?

Evil spirits.

The flaneur laughed, but over the years he has had ample reason to be glad that there is a mountain between his house and Tinker Street. From the war over Misty's at the Woodstock Guild to the current bitter fight over the library renovations, modern Woodstock has kept alive a proud record of contentiousness.

But if there were evil spirits, where did they come from ... and what did they want? Trail keeper, mapmaker and guide David Holden provided a far-fetched yet resonant answer: They want peace and quiet. His theory is that the Comeau Property was once the center of a vast necropolis of Indian dead that covered the entire village area. Perhaps they were Mohicans. Their spirits want to sleep in peace—but is this likely in a town that buries its artists separately?

The willingness—and sometimes the eagerness—to do battle that is so much a part of Woodstock's character began, perhaps, with the Anti-Rent Wars of the early nineteenth century, when thousands of locals decided they were tired of paying rent to the Livingstons, absentee landlords who lived across the Hudson. So young Woodstock men, dressed as Indians, conducted a second American Revolution, right here on Wittenberg Road.

A major component of contentiousness is the rock solid certainty that one is right, and the other fellow is not only wrong, but ... evil. In twentieth century Woodstock, artists followed the Communist party line with such unity that, according to one centenarian liberal witness, if you didn't unquestioningly follow where Stalin led, you were certain to be ostracized.

As the flaneur ambled about the village inspecting the once white remains of winter and looking for signs of spring, he was reminded of battles major and minor he had witnessed, and a few he had joined. There had been scuffles over where to put the town highway garage; the new post office, and affordable housing; the loss of the Grand Union was even deemed worthy of picketing. But the two bloodiest battles, interestingly, were waged against cultural institutions: the Woodstock Guild of Craftsmen, and the Woodstock Library.

The war between Misty's Restaurant and the Guild brought together elements of farce and nastiness. Hundreds took sides, including some of the town's most illustrious citizens—from "Woody" Broun to Jay Wenk. (Full disclosure: the flaneur, as Program Director of the Guild, was on the front lines). The issue seemed simple at the time. Misty rented a space in the Guild building, which she turned into a popular restaurant—almost a private club—for Woodstock's culturati. The Guild board decided it needed the space and gave Misty notice. It should have been cut and dried, but this was Woodstock. The sh*t hit the fan.

The feedback section of *Woodstock Times* buzzed with indignation. The battle was joined, framed as a tiny eatery vs. a giant arts organization. Long-standing friendships were ended. The flaneur was threatened with fisticuffs by a man twice his age. Picket lines marched in front of the Guild's Tinker Street building. The only spot of levity came when a photographer asked the flaneur to pose, dukes up, with Misty's supporter Jay Wenk. Instead, the two locked arms and lifted their legs in a dance step. Rancor and bitterness ruled in conversations for months. Was it something in the water? The flaneur wondered.

Eventually Misty reopened her restaurant across the street, where she was successful for many years.

Call it civic catharsis or Mohican curse, the long-ago battle over Misty's split the town in the same way the library war is doing today. Such battles are like forces of nature, like the Mediterranean wind that is said to make people want to kill.

The flaneur had a theory about the leaders of these bellicose visitations. They were smart, and they were bored. They had too much time on their hands. They paid lip service to democracy, but only if it went their way. If they desired a different outcome, for instance, than the one voted on by a democratically elected library board, they cited the sixties mantra, "Question Authority" and set about destroying public confidence in the cultural center of the Most Famous Small Town in the World. He strolled down Tinker Street, shaking his head.

On the library lawn spring was daubing things green; here and there white spots of winter refused to melt...

The flaneur relaxed in the weak March sun, on the bench purchased as a memorial to the late Ruth Simpson, the feisty half pint who'd learned how to fight in gay liberation battles of the sixties. A long-serving trustee, she was unabashedly vociferous—ferocious, in fact, when the library was under attack. But Ruth was gone. The library had its champions, but none of them had survived Stonewall....

A cold March wind made him turn up his collar. He looked out over the great lawn and blinked at the ghosts he thought he saw.

Land of the Lotus-Eaters

PEOPLE TEND TO fall in love with Woodstock, and after one visit decide to change their lives and move here. That's how it happened with the flaneur. He thought at the time that he left the city for love of a woman, or because of the mountains; but the real reason was that he was tired and Woodstock was laid back to the max—a perfect paradise for wannabe idlers, recovering workaholics, and overeducated people with time on their hands.

This revelation struck the flaneur on a beautiful Sunday afternoon in June, while ambling past the drum circle on the Village Green. It was pleasant to see adults entertaining tourists by pounding on big drums, an activity requiring no work in the way of practice, and just a scrap of talent.

The flaneur disliked work with the fervor of a fundamentalist preacher denouncing Satan and sin. It was the flaneur's opinion that humanity's fall from Eden occurred when agriculturists replaced hunter-gatherers. The shift brought war, repressive government, overpopulation, and all the evils of civilization. Because he knew that this view was so heterodox it might get him barbecued, or at least locked up in a psych ward, he kept his lip zipped. Besides, he was as ambivalent about work as he was about everything. He had worked since he was ten, when he built a shoeshine kit and started snapping a rag. The number of jobs he'd had attested to his work ethic; their variety to his being easily bored.

It struck him one day, looking around town, that Woodstock's citizens were lazy and that was why they loved to do battle with each other rather than build the library and swimming pool other towns had. For overeducated people with time on their hands, fighting was a useful substitute.

The flaneur reasoned that taking it easy was hard on people used to filling the empty hours with work. It made them nasty. Being at leisure brings you face to face with yourself, a grim prospect. The only remedy is to go forth and do good.

The flaneur sat on the Green, ignoring the din of the drumming, to think about his theory. Laziness certainly explained the shabby Coney Island look of the buildings on Tinker Street. The gardens of the Green were magnificent, but so many buildings needed a coat of paint! Having recently visited Saugerties and Rhinebeck, he knew that in towns where work was king, the streets sparkled. Even the tourists in other towns looked more prosperous.

Did they spend more?

He remembered that Woodstock stores were infamous for being unfriendly—another mark of laziness raised to the level of torpor. He got up and walked to the porch of The Woodstock Guild of Craftsmen. It had undergone a name change to focus attention on its arts colony, Byrdcliffe, and was apparently deferring maintenance on its historic Tinker Street building, which looked neglected.

The Guild porch had always provided a comfortable perch for people-watching. He recalled reading that there had once been an outdoor café on the sidewalk in front of the Guild, shaded by tall trees. What a civilized amenity an outdoor café was! Welcoming to tourists, a good place for artists to meet and talk about their work. Across the street and down a bit, there had been an outdoor café on the porch of The Center For Photography. A wonderful oasis on a summer day.

The flaneur caught himself muttering to himself. He listened—sure that no one else could hear because of the drumming—and found himself in agreement with himself: an outdoor café, not a juice bar, would do more for the arts in Woodstock than any number of schools or grants ever could. Reflecting on this positive note, he added, of course there would have to be a noise ordinance, at least on Sundays.

He realized it was hopeless. The laziness factor would prevent any improvement that would make idling more enjoyable.

Work is a curse, the flaneur intoned. It was his mantra. Only humans work. The rest of creation toils not. People came to Woodstock to chill out, but that old devil work kept jabbing them to do something—so some made noise with their hands, and some with their mouths.

When this lightbulb went off, a line of Tennyson went through the flaneur's mind. Deep Thoughts were apt to bring out the Poet: "Let us alone. What pleasure can we have / To war with evil? Is there any peace / In ever climbing up the climbing wave?"

The flaneur stood up, eyes bright with new vision. Woodstock was the land of the Lotus-Eaters. The buildings around the Green no longer looked shabby. They were perfect. They were home.

Reciting Tennyson, he walked toward the drum circle.

Pure Fun

WHEN THE FLANEUR was in his tender years, simmering up in the industrial skillet of southern Ohio, he and his cousin spent a delightfully dizzying summer driving across the state to one amusement park after another in search of scary old wooden roller coasters. When they found one, they climbed into the first car, and creaked up to high glory, savoring the way the old structure swayed. Having anesthetized themselves with swigs of white lightnin' from an old fruit jar, they didn't stop until the moon came up. Back on the ground, they staggered down the midway, gawking at the spectacle of country folk out for fun. White bucks and push-up bras were in fashion, but the flaneur and his cuz favored black motorcycle boots and tight, pegged pants. There was never much intercourse between the Hoods and the Shoulds, so they didn't try to pick up girls. They looked too serious. Back home in Dayton, the girls were more free-spirited and fun.

When winter darkness fell early, the cool kids piled into a jalopy someone had dubbed the "Deathmobile"and headed for a nearby park.

At the top of a hill they turned off the lights, put the Death-mobile in neutral, and started the blind plunge downhill which was the signal for the girls to start screaming and squirming as the jalopy gathered speed. (And so the lap dance was born....)

Pure fun in those days long ago and far away involved elements of anarchy and danger that resembled the coming of age rituals Native American boys had to undergo. Irresponsible? Absolutely. But pure fun, as opposed to the mediated kind, contains elements that would not be approved by parents and teachers. A teen's brain chemistry has yet to be stirred by the Grim Reaper—which is why they make such willing soldiers. Mortality is a word to them, not a fact. When the flaneur moved to Woodstock, the first thing he thought of when he saw Mead's Mountain Road was how much fun it would be to take a Deathmobile cruise down it. Then—being a responsible adult, he thanked God for cops.

Back in the era—forty years ago—when Woodstock law stood tall in the person of Lud (for Ludwig) Baumgarten, a strapping six-footer who fought the Japanese in Burma—oodstock was a lively music town. You could stay up till the wee hours listening to Mingus at the Lake, then drive home fully loaded, unless Lud had the night shift—he seemed to be everywhere—in which case you crept home.

Most cops put on cop faces to do their jobs. Lud was genuinely tough, the way Woodstocker Lee Marvin was in films. Lud radiated gunfighter machismo. He stood so straight the rod that ran from his oral opening to his anal pucker couldn't be bent even when he campaigned for office and had to kiss babies. The flaneur enjoyed cops because he had once worn a gold shield as a parole officer in Brooklyn. Cop humor was gallows humor. What they got away with was pure fun.

Before Lud, a single cop, Clancy, was sufficient to act as watchdog for Woodstock teen cutups. Clancy parked on the Green, where he napped and kept one eye on (among others) a boy up from East New York, Frank, who was lucky with the young ladies.

Looking back on his youth in Woodstock, Frank Spinelli, a photographer of mushrooms and the Burning Man festival, whose house on Spencer Road has a glorious view of the Ashokan Reservoir, told the flaneur a story of pure fun so innocent, so sweet, the flaneur almost went into sugar shock. Even Norman Rockwell might have had difficulty believing that such rosy-cheeked innocence was still possible in the tumultuous sixties. Pure fun back then had probably not changed since the Civil War. It seems that when a warm spring day pointed out the cruelty of compulsory education, a certain group of fun-loving Onteora students persuaded their school bus driver to stop in Shady at their favorite swimming hole. After their dip, the bus driver took them to the Village Green, where the boys teased the girls and the day ended with burgers and cokes at the counter of the News Shop—now Jean Turmo's Emporium.

Well might the patient reader ask at this point, so where's the transgression of pure fun? The flaneur smiles as he builds to the punch line. In those days, movies were shown only in Woodstock Town Hall; if kids wanted to see the latest Elvis flick, girls had to sit on one side, boys on the other. It was a strait-laced town. Rock festivals were brushed off.

So? "The swimming party was coed—and we skinny-dipped," Frank says.

I still don't get it. So what? Who were they?

"Besides me, Gilles Malkine, a popular comic, and his sister, Fern. Last but hardly least, an aspiring novelist who worked tending bar until he got the job we know him for today: Woodstock Town Supervisor Jeremy Wilber."

Oh....

Karate Kids and Kung Fu Fighting

❖ ❖ ❖ ❖ ❖

HALF A LIFETIME AGO, the flaneur was a meatloaf. He needed a makeover, big time. In the early eighties it was his habit to
sit like a bullfrog on the front porch of the Woodstock Guild and
philosophize about his wayward heft, female beauty, and the
meaning of meaning.

One fine Saturday, he noticed a troop of ten-year-olds in
white uniforms headed into the Kleinert Arts Center. They were
clean and purposeful, like Ralph Macchio in the *Karate Kid* movie
that was popular then.

Intrigued by their self-discipline, the flaneur stepped into the
Kleinert to check things out. He was immediately assaulted by a
male voice so strong it seemed roughened in the throats of a generation of gym teachers, and then polished in the vocal chords of
a Navy SEAL instructor. It was a voice that grabbed you by the
collar and threw you against the wall of your torpor. It had a charisma that made you want to please it, and a tone of command
that made obedience the only viable option.

The flaneur observed the class—calisthenics, forms, and sparring—and became a student of Korean Tang Soo Do karate.

The owner of the powerful voice was Britt St. John, and the class was a family affair: his wife Marilyn also taught. Their two young daughters were usually in attendance, demonstrating the moves in martial arts forms to kids their age.

It reminded the flaneur of dance class in sixth grade. He was clumsy then, and the years had not brought him any closer to gracefulness; but now he was twice as tall as his classmates. He was an awkward crane among white chickens, Gulliver in Lilliput. He was aware of how ridiculous he looked to the parents observing the class, but he didn't care. He was learning what the kids were learning: submission to discipline.

He slowly improved. Other adults joined the class. He didn't like sparring, but if Britt said fight, he tried out some of the punches and kicks he had practiced. His fears dissipated. But then he found himself matched with a fellow who didn't pull his punches, as Britt required. The new guy was a bully, and in fighting back, the flaneur broke a toe.

Toes heal themselves. For a time the flaneur limped around town wondering if the gain would equal the pain. A graduation ceremony was to be held in the elementary school auditorium. Each student had to break a board with his foot. There were no tricks involved. The board was real—as the embarrassment would be if he failed.

He broke the board, and a light bulb went off inside his thick skull. The lesson was about self-confidence. Courage, not fighting, was being taught. Self-discipline was an important ingredient of courage, an essential but seldom-noted aspect of our personalities, perhaps too often confused with aggressiveness. (According to surveys, our two greatest fears are public speaking and walking on a dark road.)

After four years of karate classes, the flaneur felt in good enough shape to undertake the more rigorous training in Fu Jow Pai kung fu at Mountain View Studio, with *sifu* Eric Brugnoni. A frame maker by trade, married to an artist of Japanese ancestry, Eric ran his classes with quiet authority. He taught forms, calisthenics, and light, contact sparring, assisted by imperturbable senior student Greg Dinger, who in his other life is a classical guitar player.

The flaneur kept his mouth shut and observed—as well as he could while standing with a log balanced on his outstretched forearms. The students around him were concentrated on the workout as if sitting in Zen meditation. Sweat beads dripped from foreheads. He heard stifled groans. Eric smiled.

Courage was a given in kung fu. Pain was to be ignored. The flaneur became fond of banging his forearm against that of a partner to toughen it. The bruises were displayed with nonchalant pride. After a month of training, the flaneur lost his fear of fighting. He was never very good at it, usually he could hold his own, and sometimes he got lucky like the time he knocked a giant cop down. The young officer towered over the flaneur, but the bigger they are....

Martial arts become addictive. The flaneur went to the Byrdcliffe Barn for aikido classes with Harvey Konigsberg and Lowell Miller, and spent a year studying tai chi with venerable Master T.K. Shih. Studies in Taoist fighting completed his education. Ten years passed this way.

What had he accomplished? He was in the best shape of his life, and when he walked down Tinker Street or Avenue B, he feared no evil. To celebrate, he took a solo walking trip across Wales.

Martial arts had shown him that he could live free of fear, but he could feel the ten years of work in his bones. Was he in danger of losing his idler status?

Now when he spent navel-gazing time in the philosopher's corner on the Guild porch, he daydreamed still about Schopenhauer's pitiful pessimism, and feminine pulchritude; but sometimes he just relaxed, and let his meat loaf.

⬚ ⬚ ⬚ ⬚ ⬚

Perfect Hiking Weather

⬚ ⬚ ⬚ ⬚ ⬚

WHEN AUTUMN LIGHTS the summer trees with its Indian torches, and the nightly insect orchestras have packed up for the winter, in bed, the flaneur hears the coyotes barking in his woods and remembers the fox pup spotted on the road without parental supervision. The flaneur offers a quick prayer for little brer fox. (In the past, he prayed for the deer, even those that ate his wife's garden, but there were too many of them, and too many carrying Lyme disease. Now he wishes them a quick death.)

The heat comes on in the night, and the dawn is clear and cold. Perfect hiking weather. It was going to be the kind of day when he couldn't get the mountains out of his head. The thought that he would never be able to climb up to glory again had been hard to adjust to at first, for the Catskills—and the Whites, the Sierras, and Snowdonia—had given him a great deal of pleasure when he was younger, strong, and—he had to admit it—braver. The flaneur had been a solo hiker in the mountains and had extricated himself from several dicey situations.

Those memories would have to suffice, he told himself.

One late April morning he strapped a thirty-pound pack to his back, and started up Hunter Mountain. Spring was in the air, but the cold breeze was wintry. He climbed fast, noting the skunk cabbage, and the buds on trees. Up ahead he saw a patch of white. Snow. He had not anticipated that, but he went blithely on, careful of his footing, but not alarmed.

Then he saw it. The summit of the mountain was covered with ice. He felt himself slipping, and reached out to grab a nearby striped maple. His hand slipped off the ice that sheathed it. He sat on the ground, hard—and started sliding. Using his boots as brakes, he stopped himself. He had walked into the middle of a field of ice. He couldn't turn back, and to go forward was to ride the glacier. What to do? Silence embraced him, except for the tinkling of icy branches in a slight breeze.

He took stock. He had not prepared for ice—he had not remembered that spring came late to the mountains. "A fine mess," he muttered, seeing his breath. "Let's not panic." Assessing the situation, one word came to mind: dire. Between a rock and a hard place.

All he had was his determination to survive. He had talked his way out of worse situations, but he couldn't remember what they were. A drunk capo with a gun now seemed a piece of cake next to this fix.

He decided to go forward, and to offer a running commentary on his progress to the white silence.

"One foot at a time, that's right. Keep your boots slanted, it might help a little ... take your time ..." A fall would be disastrous, a slide fatal. Slowly the flaneur talked himself across the frozen rivulets, finding a handhold here and there, crawling, all the while talking, holding on to his words like a lifeline, hypnotizing himself to keep his fear at bay. When he at last looked up, hoping to see signs of the summit, he experienced a wave of horror mixed with despair.

He faced an ice cave that he remembered from summers past. He would have to wriggle through it on his frozen hands and knees to get to the flat mountaintop, and the end of the ice. He estimated he'd been inching his way on the ice sheet for an hour. He was tired and hungry, and he was more than a little claustrophobic.

He had no choice. It was do or, most assuredly, die. He would crawl into the cave and emerge on the other side, having undergone his own Eleusinian rites. To get through, he must transcend. And so he did, inch by inch. He remembers standing at last on dry ground, sandwich in hand, looking up at the sky, imagining himself surfing on clouds, looking down at himself on the icy mountain, no bigger than an ant, as in a Chinese painting.

It was perfect hiking weather all that week. Wherever he went, the flaneur was reminded of his adventures in the mountains. Being an enthusiast when there was something to be enthusiastic about, he urged his friends and complete strangers to take a walk up in the glory while they still could. To see yourself in the landscape, small but determined, was to see yourself whole.

Good Morning Mountain

WHEN A HIKER STANDS on the summit of Overlook Mountain and looks south across the wide green Woodstock valley, he sees Ohayo Mountain, and glimpses the silvery Ashokan Reservoir behind it. This is the country the flaneur pledges allegiance to. This is Ashokan.

The flaneur has lived on the south slope of Ohayo Mountain for well over forty years, and he has walked over it nearly every day, a seven-mile round trip. When a bad fall put a hold on his peregrinations, he missed the road, so he asked his walking partner, Will Nixon, to join him, promising to reveal the secrets of one of Woodstock's more interesting thoroughfares.

When they set forth, the afternoon sun was warm, melting the dirty snowbanks that lined both sides of the road. Occasionally cars sped past, drivers trapped inside with their cell phones, chattering.

"Do you recognize people when they wave to you from their cars?" Will asked.

"I seldom look at cars," the flaneur answered. "Unless they are a threat. I can't see through tinted-glass windshields. But I confess, I look at convertibles with their tops down."

Although traffic on the road has increased, it is still possible on early mornings to climb for fifteen minutes without encountering a single vehicle. At such times the flaneur imagined other passages through thick growths of mountain laurel: a deer trail, a path for Lenape hunters, a "corduroy" road (lined with logs), up which teams of oxen pulled heavy loads of bluestone cut from the quarries below.

Once the flaneur asked the Woodstock town historian Alf Evers the origin of the name "Ohayo." Alf said that it was either Native American or a form of "Ohio" which drovers would shout. Later the flaneur was pleased to learn that "Ohio" sounds like the word for "Good Morning" in Japanese.

After they climbed the second switchback, he pointed to an unfinished garage. Next to it stood a house with a grand view of the reservoir. His friend Aileen Cramer, then in her sixties, told him that Woodstock artists would stop here for a "brew and a view." Two more switchbacks, and they passed a spot where the flaneur's favorite tree on the road once stood. He told Will that it had been a long-dead tall white birch that he never failed to memorialize on his walks to town.

Fifteen minutes of climbing brought them to the 1,388 foot summit of Ohayo Mountain. Spencer Road veers off to the right. The flaneur had a lot to say about this little-known pocket of paradise. Its cliffs afford panoramic views of the reservoir, from Kingston in the east to the mountains of the west; with the Mohonk tower a speck to the south. Named after a General Spencer, whose house commands the heights, this quiet road was once home to rock stars Maria Muldaur and Tim Hardin, and most notably to folk artist Clarence Schmidt, who looked like Santa Claus. After a fantasy castle Schmidt had built burned, his reaction was to cover his trees with tin foil. Farther down Spencer is a large house with a fine view, formerly owned by the flaneur's friends, Joe and Jane August, who left for the West Coast when Jane became a rabbi. At one time in the past, they organized a hundred of their neighbors into the Ohayo Mountain Association to fight further development on the mountain. Every summer the mountain resounds with the thumping of well drilling, as newcomers look for water that is not there (The group hired a hydrologist, who testified that—unlike the surrounding mountains—Ohayo has no catchment for rain. Water would always be in short supply.)

While the flaneur was explaining this to Will, a gaggle of wild turkeys crossed the road, strutting gracelessly like too-big-to-fail bankers on a perp walk. These old neighborhood residents seemed coyote-proof.

Directly across from the turn into Spencer is a long driveway that leads to a McMansion thrown up twenty years ago by a Florida businessman who aspired to become part of Woodstock's art scene. To this end he hired a knowledgeable dowager (and yachtswoman) to buy Woodstock art for him, and threw a fancy party for artists, who were happy to enjoy the canapés and Scotch and gape at the gold faucets in the bathrooms before telling their host that his use of water was piggish, and that it was impossible to buy into an art scene that did not exist. It's said that he sold his million-dollar house for a song not long after his party.

The summit of Ohayo Mountain was known years ago for its witch, Mrs. Grimm, who reportedly took the form of a ruffed grouse that could not be shot down by hunters. (Will took special note of this, as a ruffed grouse is in the title of one of his books.)

Back on Ohayo, they came to High Rocks Road on the left. No views, barking dogs, and the smell of money—a bank president lives at the end of that road. The stretch of Ohayo between High Rocks and Broadview reminded the flaneur of the dogs he'd encountered there. One followed him into town each time he passed, until a car ended its wandering ways. Once a man yelling behind him got his attention, shouting, "Grab him!" The flaneur turned and saw a large German shepherd galloping towards him. The flaneur is a community-minded man, but his mother didn't raise any stupid children. He stood still when the dog whooshed past, and watched the dog's owner corner him and snap a heavy leash on his collar. Panting, the man pulled the large dog over to the flaneur. "Sorry, he's wild today. He's part wolf. I guess he misses his freedom."

The flaneur restrained himself from voicing his thoughts about dog owners. Their lazy sentimentality about letting their pets run free was his number one complaint as a walker. He had seen too many fine, adventurous dogs come to sad ends.

Striding across the flat plateau, Will and the flaneur passed the homes of Hollywood producers, doctors, reggae artists, peace activists, and Woodstock's singing rabbi.

At Yerry Hill Road a large field reminds people driving by that the mountain used to be farmland. On the opposite corner Ohayo Mountain Road curves to the left to plunge downhill. Before the curve, two residences of note: that one on the right, close to the road, had been the home of Frank Meyer, a leading Conservative journalist; on the other, rock musician Tim Moore lives above the curve.

Despite a dirt road that beckons you in, a plethora of signs say "Keep Out." The property belongs to Bob Dylan. The road's best-known resident lived in a grand house once owned by Walter Weyl, founder of *The New Republic*. Below the long Dylan driveway is the house of the Russian princess, which abuts the road. It is here that the walk may briefly ascend to heaven. Will looked skeptical. The flaneur smiled. He enjoyed making jaws drop. At this point Overlook Mountain loomed before them like Mount Everest. While their feet went downhill, their eyes climbed up Overlook, creating the illusion of weightless ascension for one stunning moment.

As they headed down, the flaneur told Will stories of the mountain: the nudist colony of the sixties; the Old Farm Road house where The Band lived, and rehearsed; the farmhouse at the corner of Broadview Road, once the center of farming on Ohayo; the Lenape rock shelters; and the picket fort commanded by Elias Hasbrouck in the revolution, which had never been located. The mountain held fast to its mysteries. One of the flaneur's many character flaws was a tendency to sententiousness. He could not resist saying to Will as they parted, "The mountain has shaped me ... " But Will cut him short. "Mountains don't talk," he said.

The Republic of Ashokan

ON A COOL, OVERCAST March morning the flaneur climbed Overlook Mountain, with the intent of renewing citizenship in the Republic of Ashokan. Climbing Overlook was nothing new; he had done it dozens of times as casually as he once walked from Times Square to Washington Square. What was different was that age had crept up on him. He has become, perforce, a village saunterer, a flaneur. Could he still hike a mountain?

He had this notion, based a little on bioregionalism, and a lot on forty years residence in Ashokan—meaning the Woodstock Valley from Overlook to the reservoir—that we are first and foremost citizens of the landscape we inhabit. If you live or work in the capital of Ashokan, he thinks that every decade or so you should renew your citizenship not only by voting, but by the following: sitting through a town board meeting, volunteering, attending an art opening, sitting on the Green and watching the world go by, writing an indignant letter to *Woodstock Times*, marching in the Memorial Day Parade, climbing Overlook. (There are other, more esoteric rites)

It is altogether fitting that you should have to drive past Tibet—the huge white KTD monastery with its prayer flags hanging like the undergarments of sexy angels—on your pilgrimage to Woodstock's sacred mountain.

The flaneur pulled into the parking lot for the trailhead a few minutes after sunrise. Six cars were parked there already. His companion, Colin McKewan, is a Scot who's explored the world, its heights (he was an Outward Bound leader in the Adirondacks) and its depths (he has a masters in marine archeology).

Rain was forecast, but the clouds were parting. They started to climb. The path up Overlook is broad, graveled, and unrelenting. They talked about previous times they'd gone up this mountain, while Colin politely tried to ignore the fact that the flaneur was quietly huffing and puffing like one long-in-city pent. (The flaneur wondered, darkly, if he'd have to scrub this mission.)

They encountered Jay of Jarita's Florist and his party descending the mountain as they trudged up. Some of the people with him were older than the flaneur, and they looked like they'd been out for a stroll. Even their old dog was in better shape.

The flaneur remembered the time he'd last climbed the mountain was with another hiking buddy, the goddess Hera (aka Betty from Bearsville). Hera is famous among local hikers for leaving anyone who can't cruise at road runner speed in the dust. Hike with Hera, and mostly what you'll see of her is a blur far ahead. The woman can perambulate.

To take his mind off the climb, he told Colin the story of the ill-fated Overtook Mountain House, and then the tower behind it, which since the Eighties has blighted the nighttime. Woodstock valley with its blinking light.

Once upon a time, in recent memory, there were few houses on Overlook, at least none with the "show-off" lights that say, "look at the

97

size of the house I can afford." At night the mountain was dark. Then the tower was erected so that a Kingston TV station could broadcast *I Love Lucy* reruns. It was built by a shameless local entrepreneur who simply ignored the law against doing so—and the town fathers were asleep at the switch. Since it stood in the Albany to New York flight corridor, the FAA said it had to have a blinking light atop it.

Many citizens protested. A group was formed called "No Lights" headed, if memory serves, by attorney Alan Sussman and poet Ed Sanders. At least one rally/poetry reading was held on the summit, which drew a crowd. Earth First!-type actions were spoken of. The tower was fortified.

When the flaneur and his compatriot arrived at the ruins of the hotel he looked at his watch and was surprised to see that they'd made it up in the usual time.

He was always puzzled by the ruins that now rose before us. He could imagine the guests stepping down from the carriages that brought them up, and ascending the short flights of steps into the hotel, but what he didn't understand was how small it must have been. Of course, it was never a grand hotel like its sister, the Catskill Mountain House, but the windows are so close together it doesn't look much bigger than a typical Catskill boarding house.

They pressed on along the path that leads to the wide outcropping of rock that offers the best view of the Woodstock valley. A lone tent with no one stirring, and a cold campfire greeted them. They sat on the edge of the cliff munching breakfast and contemplating the Republic of Ashokan. There was the Hudson, a silvery ribbon to the left; there, to the south, was Ohayo Mountain.

There are many lines of thought being on a mountain may inspire. You can take stock of your life below from a "God's eye'" perspective. You can reminisce about previous hikes. You can try to imagine what the landscape was like hundreds of years ago.

(The flaneur's favorite: the great Mohawk leader, Joseph Brant, sitting on this ledge during the Revolutionary War, and deciding not to attack Woodstock.)

The flaneur's focus on this overcast morning was on the notion of home, on staying in one place, as he had for four decades— or for ten generations, as many old Woodstock families have. What keeps inhabitants of a place loyal to it? Why do we stay?

Perhaps it's as simple as the *Cheers* song: it's "a place where everyone knows your name." Maybe it's a longing for community, a place where you can contribute, where you can be a citizen whose voice is heard, and you are not just an anonymous consumer.

They started down, chatting while the flaneur ruminated. He and Colin had both been Scouts, as had most of the men he knew who loved the outdoors. He said that he thought Scouting's founder had done more for boys than anyone he could think of. Colin—usually a bright, cheery fellow—surprised him by his reply: "Yes, but today he'd probably be accused of pedophilia." They talked a little about the role of fear in our lives today, imposed upon us by politicians and the media.

Going down a mountain involves a different set of leg muscles. The front of both your thighs begins to burn. Your toes bump painfully into the toe box of your shoes.

But halfway down the flaneur no longer felt the pain. He grinned beneficently at what almost seemed like a stream of people coming up. He had done it! He was still a hiker. He had renewed his citizenship in the Republic of Ashokan.

The flaneur had seen the great world many times over. Let it go its own way. He'll stay home in his own little postage stamp of landscape, as William Faulkner called his piece of Mississippi. It is a world, and a beautiful one, spring, and the road home was yellow with forsythia.

🏵 🏵 🏵 🏵 🏵

A Walk to Kingston

🏵 🏵 🏵 🏵 🏵

I

APRIL'S BRUSH had painted the Chinese glory of forsythia on every road in Awaughkonk when the flaneur started his walk with Will Nixon to Kingston. Their destination there was the Old Dutch Church in the historic Stockade district. Their ostensible purpose was to answer a question Will had: Why did it take a century for early Dutch settlers to move out of Kingston to Zena (called Awaughkonk by Native Americans)? Was it fear of Indian attack, the fact that it was already owned by the Livingstons, or was it simply too far to walk? To find an answer to this last would require a walk. Who you gonna call?

Of course, the real reason for their trek was the fine spring day they woke to, and the chance to renew the dialogue between friends out for a little adventure. Winter was behind them, and it was time to shake a leg, and hit the open road: Route 28. They began their walk on Sawkill Road in Zena, where Morey Hill Road begins. Morey Hill is a narrow, backwoodsy road with gentle ups and downs and almost no traffic that morning. Will knew the road because he ran on it, and it was near his house. He said it had three sections: the first was the Tibetan prayer-flag neighborhood of weekenders. They passed some palatial homes and a pile of garbage dumped at the roadside. They strode along, and the conversation meandered from writing project to friendship as they passed through what Will delicately dubbed the "Northern Appalachian zone" dominated by a huge, silent dog kennel; the final third was state land, cliffs rising on one side. The flaneur was lost in pleasant reverie when Will jolted him with the news that he had taken up boxing. Now, having studied martial arts for ten years himself, the flaneur was well aware of the benefits to be gained. But Will is not the martial sort. The flaneur was absorbing this news when a Stygian roar drowned out birdsong and conversation ... they had arrived at the daily racetrack, Route 28.

They emerged from Morey Hill next to a strip of buildings that includes a pizza parlor and Five Star Exteriors. It was the stretch of the highway where giant holes are gouged in the landscape, taxes are prepared, car are washed, and billboards proliferate. If you're on foot, you wonder how you got yourself in a situation where you feel like a cowboy without his horse in the midst of a cattle stampede.

The flaneur and Will started walking, hugging the side of the road and trying to continue their conversation. Road walking makes you feel vulnerable and eccentric. Driving, you hardly notice what you're passing through. The radio's on, you may be talking or texting and you don't notice the generic ugliness. It could be Paramus. But you usually notice someone on foot. They always look poor. To be car-less in America is to be rock-bottom poor.

As they walked facing traffic, the flaneur watched carefully, on high alert, painfully aware that just one swerve by an inattentive motorist, and they were roadkill. Under these circumstances—one eye on traffic, the other on his footing—talking was choppy, but they made an effort to be heard over the constant roaring of the river they'd stepped into.

The question they asked themselves was why they were walking here rather than exploring some Catskill trail? If early settlers feared Indian attack, for sure they would have turned tail at the sight of the semis roaring by. The flaneur reminded Will that every spring for many years he had walked from his house in Glenford to Kingston, making it in three hours. "What," he shouted over the din, "was the point?" "That we can be independent of cars I guess. A symbolic gesture." It was the flaneur's standard answer. Will didn't buy it. "But people don't want to be independent of their cars. They love them." A school bus clattered by.

II

"YOU'RE CRAZY!" exclaimed Carl, the white-haired former MD who manages Half Moon Books on North Front Street in Uptown Kingston. "You can't even drive that road, much less walk it." Will had just informed Carl and store owner Jessica DuPont of their walk from Zena to Kingston on Route 28. Will and the flaneur weren't exactly certifiable, but they would admit to being a trifle tetched. It was the kind of spring day that gets pressed into the memory book, and it might have been spring fever that prompted their little adventure as much as the desire to answer a question: Why had it taken Dutch settlers a century to move into Woodstock? The flaneur also wanted to demonstrate that it was possible to go between towns on foot—not that anyone would want to. But he hoped that their walk might inspire drivers to think about the carbon dioxide they're spewing into the atmosphere, and either drive less, car pool, or use the excellent UCRT buses.

While walking 28 the flaneur thought of the train that once carried passengers from Kingston to West Hurley and points west. The tracks still ran beside the highway. He had walked them to Kingston several times, an arduous but pleasant passage high-stepping over rotting wooden ties and tall weeds. In the days when the Ulster & Delaware ran, he imagined men on horseback and teams of oxen pulling heavy wagons laden with bluestone and timber. Route 28 was a narrow, winding country road. Then in the fifties it was straightened, widened and dynamited into the racetrack it is today. A few sections of Old Route 28 remain in Glenford, charming reminders of a slower time.

They crossed the bridge over the New York State Thruway and arrived at the roundabout. When the flaneur felt the need to run in order to cross safely, he knew this would be his last walk to Kingston. He confessed to being spooked. He didn't feel safe until his Merrells slapped down on the bluestone sidewalks of Uptown Kingston.

Strolling those beautiful, quiet streets, which retain much of the character and charm of the seventeenth century, a light bulb went off—or, rather, a lamp began to glow—in the flaneur's head. Uptown Kingston, now and then, was delightful. For the colonists, the grass was not necessarily greener in Awaughkonk. There had been no incentive to leave home, and hack a farm out of the wilderness. They passed the county courthouse and crossed the street to Kingston's cathedral, the Old Dutch Church, founded in 1659 and rebuilt as it is now in 1852. The flaneur stood with Will leaning on the wrought iron fence that surrounds the church and its cemetery, which contains the bones of seventy Revolutionary War patriots. In the sparkling noon sun the huge pile of stone seemed to suck up the light. (The famous architect Calvert Vaux said of it "I cannot change a thing without impairing the exquisite unity. It's ideally perfect.")

Like the courthouse down the street, the church possessed a solidity and beauty that anchored the city. "You know what?" the flaneur said to Will. "Maybe the Dutch settlers who are buried here were happy with their lot. Why go pioneer someplace new if you think you've got it made where you are?" Will nodded. "Maybe the proof of this is the Dutch Reformed Church in Woodstock. When they did move, they recreated what made them feel comfortable." Did the flaneur and Will have their answer? Maybe. Speculating about the past is interesting, but ultimately fruitless. Those who came before took their secret motivations with them.

The flaneur and his walking partner sat down to lunch at Deising's to continue their discussion. If the early Dutch stayed where they were because they were content, they were un-American; for today movement is everything. The open road—28 in this case—offered the illusion of freedom. The problem with this is familiar: Wherever you go, there you are. On the road only the walker is truly free. The road stretches before him, and he must go down it under his own steam. When he arrives at his destination he is subtly changed. He had learned something about himself. His freedom has been his self-reliance.

Having settled this little problem to their satisfaction, the flaneur walked out into the sunshine, where he and Will were pleased to find a car waiting for them.

A Parking Problem?

SOMETIMES THE FLANEUR likes to sit on the Village Green and watch the cars go by. He amused himself similarly growing up on the banks of the Ohio—even going so far then as to write down license plate numbers. Cars intrigued him—their smells, their noises. He loved to sit on their running boards. He admired their hood ornaments. There is a photo of him, aged six, as part of the pit crew for his cousin's entry in a soapbox derby. Mainly, cars fascinated him because of their hold on people. He liked cars well enough, and would have many reasons to love them over the years, but he could do without them.

Most people couldn't. Not because a car is a necessity, but because it had become part of them, like a hand, a leg, or a cell phone. As the flaneur watched the traffic flow around and past the Green, he imagined the cars as living beings—horses, looking for a hitch. We don't drive cars—they drive us. They need a place to wait. Parking had become a problem in Woodstock.

Not a real problem—there's still plenty of open ground dedicated to parking—two huge lots in the town center, plus

Houst's lot, and two on the Comeau. (Bradley Meadows and the CVS lot are a bit of a stretch, but if you're not elderly or infirm, get some exercise.)

No, parking isn't a real problem, but a perceived problem, that started with the library annex controversy. No, there's not enough parking at the library. Never has been. So what? Park and walk. That's why you live in a small village, right?

Over the years, the flaneur has given a lot of thought to the love affair people have with their cars, and he has given up attempting to change anyone's mind. Mass hypnosis has been injected into human DNA. The flaneur anticipated the birth of the first baby born with tires instead of feet. He thought the tires would have to be truck tires to carry the weight of a sedentary, obese population. He chuckled, and looked to see if anyone nearby had heard. Sitting on the Green in many people's minds was a sign that you had lost your marbles; chuckling to yourself was asking for a butterfly net.

The man formerly known as Jogger John was sweeping the Green. These days John rode a bicycle, but he was always active, and as a result, in great shape.

The flaneur wanted to ask John if he thought Woodstock had a parking problem, but that worthy citizen seemed to be in a meditative trance leaning on his broom, so the flaneur decided to pose his question to another Senator of the Streets, the Ghost of Mark.

Mark departed Tinker Street for the next world awhile ago. A former patent attorney, Mark had thrown himself into the town's problems, holding forth on street corners about where to locate the new post office, and other civic matters of small moment to most.

The flaneur asked the Ghost of Mark about cars, and the G of M offered a cryptic reply, as ghosts are wont to do.

"Peak oil."

The flaneur pondered this reply. It didn't have the same dramatic impact as "Nevermore," from Poe's raven, but the flaneur got the message. The G of M was reminding the flaneur of a discussion about cars they'd had once. The gist was that the world was mainlining oil to support a car habit that was devastating the earth, and the only hope of stopping it was to run out of oil. Peak oil meant that the production of oil had peaked some time back, and soon we would be running on fumes. The question was, how soon?

The traffic rolling past the Green was endless. The flaneur thought of the time he'd spent trying to warn people of the dangers of the car cult. He'd gotten exactly nowhere. Peak oil would end—if the G of M was right—the cancerous growth of the infernal combustion industry. But that could take a lifetime. Meanwhile, where would an increasing number of drivers park when they came to town? Giving more open acreage to the family flivver was out of the question....

Then it came to him. What lay in his town's future was a...parking garage! He laughed, loudly. The man formerly known as Jogger John looked sharply at him as if reading his mind, and smiled.

In Woodstock there is never a problem without an absurd— or at least an extreme—solution.

Confessions of a Walker

THE TIME HAD COME. It was his birthday, and the flaneur had to renew his driver's license. He went to the Department of Motor Vehicles in Kingston's glass menagerie, but instead of renewing his right to roll down the road, he applied for a New York State ID, a walker's license.

After a lifetime behind the wheel, the flaneur voluntarily gave up his right to put the pedal to the metal. The first thing to be said about this radical act is that now the roads will be a little safer. He was not a good driver. How can you be when you're terrified? Forty years ago, he had driving lessons from a crazy instructor who took him to Fifth Avenue and Fifty-seventh Street at evening rush hour and said, "sink or swim." He survived and got his license, but felt like a fraud. Next to him, Mr. Magoo was Dale Earnhardt. The flaneur couldn't believe that a sane society would let him join the lemming herds on the Interstates. He was able to shirk his driving duties for years, but then he moved to Woodstock. He had kids who needed to go places. He drove.

And so it began—the full catastrophe. His long history with used cars and garages in Woodstock. His friend Rush Harp, the rotund "assassinologist," sold him his first junker, a fifties Chevy. (It helped that Rush guaranteed that he would "Rush to the rescue" if it broke down.) A dozen examples of rusting Detroit iron sat in the flaneur's driveway over the years, the most notable being a black sixties Fleetwood Cadillac limousine with red leather interior and a bar in the back. Fins. When he looked out at that beauty, he fantasized that the president was visiting. He was inspired not to drive it, but to polish it.

In the seventies Woodstock was really a music town. Bars and clubs could afford to offer bands because people drank and then drove. Tough DWI enforcement put a stop to that.

The flaneur was stopped once when driving the Caddy erratically. He handed the officer his license and was let off with a warning. Whew! It was only when he got home and found that the folded twenty dollar bill tucked behind his license for emergencies was missing that the flaneur realized to his horror that he had perhaps innocently, inadvertently, bribed a cop.

The flaneur won't miss the care and feeding of automobiles. It always seemed that owning a junker was at least as much trouble as owning a horse. If it hadn't been for gruff, red-faced Ken Reynolds, who owned Ken's Exxon (now a pizza parlor) on Mill Hill Road, the town would have come to a stop. In the seventies, old Ford Falcons, Dodge Darts, and VWs filled the parking lots at the Grand Union and the A&P, each one carefully nursed with oil, transmission fluid, and antifreeze. People bought recap tires and changed to snow tires and chains in the winter. Even the flaneur could open up a car hood and identify what he was looking at.

In winter, dead batteries were a problem. How many icy mornings did he call Ken to come with his wrecker? And how many times did he refuse the flaneur's money with a growl and a wave of his oil-stained hand?

People talk about the freedom their cars offer them. They can go anywhere they want. Enclosed in their box on wheels they can escape the pressures of daily life. For adolescents, getting a car at sixteen is a right of passage into adulthood. Vroom!

The flaneur has always thought of cars as balls and chains. Driving is slavery; walking is freedom. The long walks he's taken proved he could go anywhere he wanted on foot: across Wales, down the Cornwall coast, across the island of Tobago; daily, over Ohayo Mountain—and once a year to prove a point—a walk down Route 28 from Glenford to the Kingston Mall.

The ethical questions raised by driving are studiously ignored by the staunchest of environmentalists. The thirst for oil blackens the land and sea, causes most wars, pollutes, despoils, and—the flaneur could go on, but what's the point? Our addictive love for the internal combustion engine is terminal and suicidal. Women in Black: Want to end war? Stop driving! Anti-frackers: Start walking! Occupiers: Want to win economic justice? Stop driving! Walking is subversive and revolutionary.

Driving is the most dangerous thing most of us will ever do. We piously express our outrage at gun violence, then blithely tool down the road in loaded weapons, weaving in and out of traffic, failing to signal—even the most mild-mannered, law-abiding sober citizen sometimes drives like an aggressive drunk.

The result is forty thousand traffic fatalities a year. The question is not why the flaneur is a scaredy-cat, but why more drivers aren't terrified. He knows the arguments: How would you get to work without cars? (Fine and dandy for you to espouse a revolution that might actually save the planet, but we have to be practical.)

Here are the flaneur's car keys. He's opting out of the rat race. He knows it's selfish to put on others the responsibility of getting his carcass where he needs to go, but his wife loves to drive, friends are kind, and bus drivers need passengers.

And there's always shank's mare.

Lady H and the Missing Dinosaurs

ONCE, DINOSAURS ROAMED NEW YORK. Not long ago they were so numerous herds of them clogged the highways, morning and night. They invariably dressed in armor, even at home—wearing hats and suits, and responsible expressions on serious faces. Many of them had lived through the Great Depression, and fought in Korea, the South Pacific, and Europe. They had shown their mettle in combat, and returned home to take charge. Their reign seemed eternal. Then, one day in the sixties, they vanished. The Real Grown-Ups disappeared. The Children's Crusade had hit them like a comet slamming into Earth.

A shadow fell across the land. The word went out that Real Grown-Ups were no longer needed. Youth (white, prosperous) celebrated with music festivals ... and drugs. Everyone felt equal and entitled. Everyone dressed the same—like teens, in T-shirts and jeans. Everyone stayed stoned. When the formerly Real Grown-Ups emerged from their hiding places, they wore pony tails and mutton-chop-style facial hair, and they wanted to do a doobie with their supercilious offspring.

The world had turned upside down.

For a while drugs, sex, and rock and roll ruled. Naturally, the celebrants blew it when they discovered that freedom was another name for responsibility.

Such were the idle thoughts in the pinball machine that passed for the flaneur's mind as he sat on a hard bench on the Village Green contemplating a newspaper headline about a heroin epidemic in the World's Most Famous Small Town. (Now that his PD had hobbled him, and he could not roam the byways of his Village, a bench on the Green had become his observation post on Woodstock). When he sat still, he was invisible. It was early spring, midmorning in April.

The flaneur knew heroin by many fanciful names. In the sixties poet friends in the East Village preferred "Lady H." They shot up in his bathroom. One night, he recalled, he had been persuaded to taste Lady H in a glass of wine. Hot liquid silk had filled him with a certainty he had never before experienced. The world was perfect, and pain free, and he belonged in it. This was followed by another certainty: that he must never taste Lady H again. He was too susceptible to her charms.

Was it a coincidence that a few weeks later, he accepted a job as a New York State Narcotics Parole Officer? He was not a narc, he told his friends. He was assigned the impossible job of finding jobs for junkies. But he had made arrests, and he had taken people to jail. When he learned that he had been hired to enforce the savagely racist Rockefeller drug laws, he turned in his badge.

As he mused that some of the junkies he had watched enter prison would be getting out now, an old Toyota pulled up to the curb just yards away from where he sat. The passenger-side window rolled down, a paper bag was handed to a boy in a football jersey, and the deal was done—so blatantly the flaneur looked around for cops. They had always kept an eye on the Green. No longer.

So this was the epidemic that was making headlines. The story the flaneur read covered the waste of young lives and sketched the economics of junk, but the writer did not venture into the dark country of why? Why were so many people who had grown up in this mountain paradise—who lived, when compared with, say, the millions of refugees now flooding into Europe, like princes of the blood—looking, at the start of their lives, for an emergency exit?

Was the answer somehow related to the loss of the Real Grown-Ups? Had the zeitgeist become so frightening that voters might really elect Conan the Barbarian president of the strongest nation in the world? Like the "Just Say No" campaign of yore, the feeble, ineffectual community efforts undertaken against heroin couldn't compete against what Lady H offered: oblivion. If the reality of that was too stark for most to accept, consider what else she offered: a way of life that demanded your full attention 24/7. No hassles of responsibility, relationship, or career, no entanglements except with Lady H. Chasing her was both your career and vocation.

Serve her, and you were free. You belonged to a secret society, whose members had only to show the track marks on their bodies to be welcomed by other vipers. In other words, you could remain a kid.

The flaneur shook his head. What kids needed more than anything else was a rite of passage that would earn them the respect of their community. It was why thousands of kids from around the world flocked to become soldiers for ISIS. This drive of young men to prove their manhood seemed universal. Boys needed to show themselves worthy to enter adulthood. Give them roles to play or they would destroy themselves.

In other times the gatekeepers of adulthood had been called Real Grown-Ups because they were seemingly wise (or at least mature) authority figures—"Father Knows Best" types. They kept the world safe while kids slept. They could be counted on to do the right thing.

Like the tooth fairy, it was a nice fantasy. Unlike the dinosaurs that vanished, the myth of the Real Grown-Ups was just that: a myth. Any bright teenager would have learned that the world was not run by the competent and mature, but by the mean and mad. The twentieth Century had been the most murderous in human history, claiming one hundred and eighty-seven million fatalities in a series of bloodbaths. There was no hiding the nature of the reptilian brain in the human animal.

The flaneur stood, and stretched. In an hour on the bench, he had considered every facet of an intractable problem. There were no good answers, but the only approach that offered any realistic hope at all, he concluded, was legalization.

Ching! His mental pinball machine lit up with telepathic protest, from families who had lost children to Lady H to would-be Real Grown-Ups, those who believed in punishment, to those who hoped rehab might yet work.

Lady H is strong and seductive, with a hypnotic appeal to those who are overwhelmed by fear and pain. Kids are no match for her, but perhaps, the flaneur hoped, legalization was the most efficacious way to save them.

Different Strokes

DESPITE THE TITLE, this is not a story about sex. How could it be? It takes place in Woodstock, and everyone knows Woodstock Is Not Sexy. But back in 1972, when the flaneur blew into town, it sizzled. In fact—in the argot of that time—it was smokin', brother. Passion galore. Of course, we were young then.

As foolish as he is today, the years have wised up the flaneur—somewhat. Back then, he was a complete fool, a victim of the cockamamie idea that love and sex are one. The woman he followed to Woodstock had been here for a year before he joined her. On his second night in town she threw a party to welcome him. She had a lot of friends, mostly male. (After all, it was still the sixties, and she was a free spirit.) The flaneur called her other names, but here she will be Mora. Her T-shirt said it all: "So many men, so little time." She wanted more.

She was standing in the middle of her small living room greeting her guests with deep kisses. They sat on the floor. When one of them ran his hands up her bare leg and under her short skirt, Mora looked down at him, smiled, saw the flaneur's long face, and stepped away.

The man sitting cross-legged looked like a folded-up giraffe. His name was Les Crook, one of the most extraordinary—and tallest—men ever to lope down Tinker Street. He is long gone from the Village Green—where at the time of their up-skirt meeting he had a macrobiotic restaurant, and across Tinker, a bookstore—but for the flaneur, Les and his friend Peter Blum embodied the creative spirit of Woodstock at its fecund best. The flaneur's initial jealousy turned into amused admiration as, over the years, he came to know Les and Peter.

That winter was quiet. People stayed home. The town rolled up the sidewalks and dogs slept in the streets. The snowplows growled overtime, and often the flaneur would have the library to himself. No electronic hum warned him that the future arrived. He studied Woodstock history on the Woodstock shelf, and read firsthand recollections of past times by art colony founders, looking for what had drawn them to the village, and what kept them here. After a decade in Manhattan, he'd had his fill of hustle, noise, and crime; of too many people, and way too many buildings. He was hungry for mountains and trees, and for something he had not found in New York: the companionship of like-minded people, especially those who had glimpsed freedom through the cracked windows of the sixties.

The flaneur in those days would walk a mile for a laugh—make that two miles, for it was his fate to walk to and fro on the earth—and he would go a mile for a toothy smile. Les had a cable television program which he used to skewer political correctness and barbecue crisp black the most egregious sacred cows of that era. Lenny Bruce and the Firesign Theatre of *Don't Crush that Rodent—Hand Me The Pliers* were similarly acquired tastes. Les changed his name to Les Visible, and ended up in the Black Forest of Germany, where he became a country and western singer, and published an occult detective novel. Always surprising, Les Visible is doubtlessly keeping an eye on us from above. The flaneur looks forward to greeting him when his UFO lands.

Although Les was gone, the remaining personalities left pursuing their personal visions were hard to keep up with. Marco Vassi played a leading role in more than one area. He founded Metamonkey Video, which broadcast from the center of town in challenge to Ken Marsh's monopoly on experimental video. Overnight, everyone had a video camera.

Marco's girlfriend Evelyn Honig was connected to the English avant-garde. She brought news of John Michell, author of *View Over Atlantis*, espousing the idea that "ley lines" with mystical meanings covered the British Isles. (He also had the notion that the best high was achieved by boring a hole in your skull.)

The flaneur's skull remained intact, as did his memories. It was a memorable time, with gurus on every corner, drugs easily available, AIDS unheard of, and tolerance, a given.

People followed their bent without hindrances. In the absence of DWI fervor, late night music flourished. Orgies were discreet, as were nudist camps and hot tubs. People gave peace a chance, as well as adultery.

On one memorable evening there was a poetry reading at the Three Penny Café (where the health food store is now) and a mystery guest appeared, calling herself M'amselle. This remarkable self-creation was one of Manhattan's leading dominatrices. Tall, beautiful, imperious, she had sung opera, and now she wanted to be a poet. She had long red hair and beautiful enunciation, but scant talent. She later edited *Penthouse Forum*, and after that—became librarian of a Manhattan seminary.

M'amselle's appearance at the Three Penny Café marked a high point in seventies Woodstock. It was somehow innocent, marked with an American sincerity still occasionally found in flyover country. What followed her was a phenomenon: Woodstockers dressed in orange, with malas around their necks, the teachings of a rascally guru—Rajneesh—on their lips, and blessed lust in their hearts.

And then came AIDS....

Geezerhood

AGE DIMINISHES US. One minute we're fifty, which the French say is the youth of aging, and the next we're seventy, looking at a stranger in the mirror. Geezerhood has struck, and the youth culture demands our disappearance. If we lived in China, we would be venerated as Living National Treasures, treasured for our wisdom. Here, we're in the way.

It was a cold day in hell when this unhappy assessment appeared on the scream screen in the flaneur's mind. Being negative about anything makes him shiver. Accepting what is with good grace was his strategy for catching up to Methuselah, but he was fed up with being exhorted to get out of youth's way. Like everyone in a conformist society, he tried to cover up the tread marks of age that made indentations in his formerly open physiognomy. He curbed the curmudgeon that paced inside. But life has four seasons, and spring, however sweet, does not last forever. Winter is tart, but tasty, if you can keep warm and well fed.

The national news was full of stories about "seniors" (a PC term he hated, preferring the honesty of "old") taking all the available jobs and housing and sucking up Social Security funds. The Boomers who could not afford retirement in Death's Waiting Room, aka Florida, stubbornly remained in place and Juniors resented their longevity. (Although thankful for a parental roof.)

So the old, if not despised, are given short shrift by those who, by keeping fit, hope to grow old. Death might come at any moment from cradle to grave, but old people have survived to grow gray. As the Chinese say, the old have eaten without themselves being eaten—proof enough of their wisdom.

The flaneur had known two Woodstockers who had shown him by example how to grow old without scaring the horses: the historian Alf Evers, and the painter William Pachner. Together, the flaneur and Alf assembled the giant two-week Woodstock Bicentennial Celebration, and gave guided tours of Byrdcliffe. They even appeared in tandem on television.

Attaining a successful geezerhood does not come automatically. There is a learning curve, a Geriatrics 101, in which the first lesson is surrender: You can no longer do what you could do just last year. Accept this change, and throw yourself into something you can do. Don't retire—begin a new project. Having finished his doorstopper volumes on the history of Woodstock and the Catskills, at an advanced age Alf Evers started his last book, on the history of Kingston. This good advice is seldom followed, although often cited. Retirement is risky.

When Alf wasn't writing, he was talking. If you asked him a question about local history, it was best to put aside at least ten minutes for the answer. History is memory, and Alf's memory was prodigious, so complete that the flaneur thought of him as Alf the Memorian. He was a totemic figure around town in his nineties, drawing SRO crowds when he spoke at a Library Forum. His grandfatherly look was that of the archetypal storyteller.

There is a price to be paid for remaining above ground longer than most. Both Alf Evers and Bill Pachner lost their eyesight. The last time the flaneur saw Alf, he was presiding over an annual gathering in a natural amphitheater above his house. Music and Alf: a good time in the secret Woodstock. Later it was learned that the couple who brought him to the party forgot to guide him down. Uh oh.

Bill Pachner will turn one hundred this spring. He had to stop painting decades ago when he lost his sight, but he had a one man show at the Kleinert not long ago, and on that occasion gave a talk to a large crowd of artists which demonstrated that he still has all his marbles. Unlike Alf, Bill has a sarcastic streak, his motto being "Sincerity when necessary. Honesty when possible."

When the flaneur pays a call on his oldest friend, they often speak of the books Bill "reads" with audio aids. Bill keeps up intellectually. His memory, like Alf's, is encyclopedic.

Recently, he referred to his age, which he seldom does. "I am reluctant to claim enlightenment, but some days I think I am. It's only taken a century to get here."

He shook hands, and made his usual joke: "Goodbye, please."

Some Still Sing
—Portrait Of An Artist on His Hundredth Birthday

OLD AGE BRINGS a few sweet blessings and a plethora of curses. Everyone wants to live forever, but no one wants to be old. The old are, to say the least, inconvenient: slow in the fast lane; wise maybe, but not clever. Nevertheless, when a geezer turns one hundred, we want to know his secrets for long life. "How seemly then"—to quote W.H. Auden—for the flaneur to visit his oldest friend on the rainy April afternoon when he marks his hundredth birthday.

William Pachner was born in Bohemia in the last days of the Austro-Hungarian Empire, when Franz Joseph was Emperor, a vanished world preserved in the architecture of Vienna and the novels of Joseph Roth and Robert Musil.

He has lived in his house on Ohayo Mountain Road since 1952.

For this momentous occasion Bill's son Ned had flown in from California, joining his sister Ann, a New York artist who has a summer place nearby. While waiting for the birthday boy to appear, the flaneur sat with the Pachner progeny in a tiny dining room with windows offering a magnificent view of the Devil's Path mountains—the northern wall of Ashokan.

The flaneur asked Ned about growing up in Woodstock in the fifties, when his best friend was Chevy Chase, one of the original stars of "Saturday Night Live."

Bill appeared before Ned could answer the flaneur's question about Woodstock's SNL star. Although the years have stolen Bill's sight and hearing, he moves in his own house with cautious confidence. His mind is brightly lighted, with every memory in place, and his sarcastic wit can still stab and singe. A decade ago he was a dandy, dressed in brightly colored duds with an ascot at his neck. Now he's casual—his hair is uncombed, and he wears sweatpants. Tea is served, and Bill talks. Since he cannot understand the flaneur's speech (it has to do with timbre, not volume) Ned must interpret.

"I suppose you want to know my secret for longevity."

"Sheer cussedness?" the flaneur ventured, and waited for Ned to relay his question. His voice boomed in the small room. Bill nodded, staring sightlessly out the window in the direction of Overlook. "That's right. Will power."

Bill ignored snappy comebacks, but the flaneur knew he appreciated them. Willpower—desire—was a favorite subject in their talks. After a friendship of forty years, shorthand is developed. The flaneur had learned that, in the aggressive verbal sparring that filled the gaps in their weekly conversations, he must give as good as he got. Sometimes he had to be a counterpuncher in their conversational clinches.

One of the reasons Bill willed himself to make it to the century mark was the murder of his entire family—some eighty souls—

by the Nazis. It fell to him to avenge them as he could—with his art. From his early magazine illustrations to his later black and white paintings, Bill memorialized victims of the Holocaust. (St. Petersburg, Florida's Holocaust Museum gave him a major retrospective on his ninetieth birthday.)

Bill believes in fate. He scoffs at the regimens of exercise and diet centenarians often recommend as recipes for long life. But the flaneur has seen his friend spend hours daily on his hands and knees, manicuring his lawn. He listens to serious audio books night and day. Two years ago he agreed to be "interviewed" by the flaneur during a show of his work at the Kleinert. A large crowd listened raptly as he spoke about art in an extemporaneous monologue so perfectly phrased the flaneur had nothing to add.

Bill's features at one hundred are hawklike, aristocratic in the way those of the painter Balthus were at the end of his life. His humor is delivered with a straight face, as in the story he tells of the wealthy cartoonist J.P. McEvoy, who owned Woodstock Estates. His wife was so small that when she took a spin you jumped because it looked like no one was behind the wheel.

As a student in Prague he told everyone he wanted to work for *Esquire*. Ten years later he became its art director. He escaped the fate of his family because he'd come to America to pursue his dream. He looked at the flaneur with his we-are-guided-by-unseen-forces look, then stared off into space, shaking his head. "The things I've seen ... the things I've seen...."

Born in another time, he had survived the violence and the cataclysmic changes of the twentieth century. He had succeeded in creating a facsimile of his Bohemian birthplace on Ohayo Mountain; he had made the leap from illustrator to serious artist. One afternoon he had surprised the flaneur by remarking, "It's taken a century, but I think I might have achieved enlightenment." This started the flaneur pondering why some people live so much longer than the norm. He put his thoughts into a paragraph he asked Ned Pachner to read to his father on his birthday:

"In the cage of age we rattle the bars that confine us, we tug at the chains that tether us. Confinement comforts us with the illusion of safety. If we are being kept alive, it must be for a reason. We have value in the eyes of gods unknown, some usefulness perhaps; a beauty still in bloom that we are blind to, a charm that will not fade. Perhaps it is the music that we make that pleases, and keeps us, singing, alive. In the cage of age we pace out our immemorial destinies, dreaming in our senescence of release, and of a freedom we never knew. Our hands weaken on the bars we built, on the chains we forged, hoping they will hold. Into the night we howl, while the moon smiles upon our tribute, and some still sing."

Seekers and Extraordinary Woodstockers

THERE'S SOMETHING about Woodstock that attracts spiritual seekers. From Tibetan and Zen Buddhists to Breatharians—not to speak of long established churches and a synagogue—the town draws those looking for immanence and hoping for enlightenment. The flaneur has known many of them. Herewith, quick sketches to memorialize friends.

The Erotic Novelist

THE EROTIC NOVELIST and erstwhile Maitreya buddha Marco Vassi lived in Woodstock for over a decade, Byrdcliffe to Bearsville. In 1970 he had a room at the Tannery Brook Motel, where the flaneur would stop to visit him on his daily walk to town.

Marco had a gift of gab that could be entrancing; his conversation ranged from the metaphysical to the sexual. He aspired to guruhood, but his real recognition came from his writing. (*The New York Times* called him "the new Henry Miller.") He attracted acolytes and girlfriends with his charisma. He spun verbal castles in the air punctuated with winning giggles.

"Save me from women who care for me," he said. "I'm trying desperately to become a homosexual. I have so far detached from reality, I'm permanently mad. It's a joyous state if I can control my breathing."

Marco called himself a "male lesbian," but none of this ambiguity hurt his attraction for the opposite sex. Even when he stirred up a feminist hornet's nest with his controversial *Woodstock Times* column, "The Divine Path Of Growing Old," women pursued him.

He published dozens of books, including one of the best memoirs of the sixties, *The Stoned Apocalypse*; and he washed dishes at The Bear Café.

Marco didn't achieve the guruhood he sought in Woodstock, but he did have a good time here. He died of AIDS in 1989. Norman Mailer spoke of his literary significance at a memorial for him attended by dozens of girlfriends. The flaneur helped scatter his ashes in Magic Meadow.

The Sannyasin

WHEN THE FLANEUR was young in New York he would sometimes encounter a tall bearded man in Viking regalia standing silent vigil on Sixth Avenue. The flaneur often thought of this iconic figure, whose name was MoonDog, when he encountered Mark standing sentinel on Mill Hill Road. Like MoonDog, Mark remained at his post in all weathers, seldom speaking, almost never smiling. Who was this grubby Diogenes, this short, bearded, unhealthy-looking street denizen? Was he mentally ill, or some kind of holy man?

Born Harvey Rogosin, Mark had been a patent attorney, traveled the world, and left behind a wife and daughter and a Fifth Avenue apartment when he moved to Woodstock. Sometimes he seemed crazy, and needed to be cared for, and sometimes he was crazy like a fox. His refuge was the Woodstock Library, where his friend, librarian D.J. Stern, welcomed him into her office.

He got excited about local controversies like the closing of the Grand Union and the siting of the (then) new post office, and would sit at the computer writing letters. Mark was fussed over by his friends, who worried about his health. The flaneur watched people's reactions to him. If they turned up their noses, they probably weren't worth talking to.

If he liked you, Mark would give you a rock on which he'd painted an "Om" in Sanskrit; this might be accompanied by a thumbs-up.

Mark was a sannyasin—one who has left everything behind in order to pursue his spiritual needs. His silent street corner vigils reminded the flaneur and many others of the world beyond worlds many seek.

The Handyman

NOT SO LONG AGO, the term "Woodstock carpenter" was a punch line, referring to a feckless fellow who'd rather be picking a guitar than wielding a hammer. You couldn't trust him to show up on time, or to do a competent job.

Ed Kossoy changed that image. When the flaneur got to know him, Ed worked Mondays at the Woodstock Library. A roofer, carpenter, and handyman, Ed was punctual, and could figure out how to fix anything. Meanwhile, he talked. Ed loved to talk, and the flaneur listened. Bronx born, Ed had worked as a cab driver and as an attendant at Payne-Whitney; when he came to Woodstock he had an import-export business. He told good stories about his experiences, but above all he liked to talk about food. Ed tried every restaurant in the Mid-Hudson region, and the results were posted in his midriff. A close second to his dining experience was his spiritual quest, which for a long while was centered on a Buddhist retreat in High Falls.

Ed's main teacher, however, was G.I. Gurdjieff. He read the books written about the Master by those who had been close to him, and he could talk "the work" by the hour—while getting his own work done. He seemed to have no ego attachments. He was honest, kind, and friendly. The flaneur viewed him up close for nine years, and he thought that while not a guru, Ed was the closest he had ever come to knowing someone truly enlightened.

Ed died suddenly in 2012.

The Grande Dame

AILEEN CRAMER was one of the last of Woodstock's grand dames. The daughter of jut-jawed artist-photographer Konrad Cramer and artist Florence Ballin Cramer, Aileen was Woodstock aristocracy. Her white hair and regal bearing, combined with a background in theatre, gave her a formidable aspect. The flaneur couldn't help falling for her. Sometimes they climbed Mount Guardian together, or cleared trails there. On fine summer mornings, they might go for a drive in her sporty Karmann-Ghia convertible, which was graced with freshly-cut flowers in a vase.

Aileen served, noblesse oblige, on the boards of the town's leading arts organizations, as well as the town board. The flaneur watched her shock fellow board members by simply speaking her mind. This is a rare thing these days, and it can be intimidating or endearing, depending on your strength of character.

It was Aileen who taught the flaneur that a true Woodstocker enjoys a love-hate relationship with his hometown. Toward the end of her long life Aileen announced that she was "ready to go." Shortly thereafter, she went.

Supreme Assassinologist

RUSH HARP called himself an assassinologist. He was obsessed with what he considered to be a conspiracy surrounding JFK's murder in Dallas. Other than this crotchet, he was as normal as any retired IBM-er with some bucks might be. When the flaneur stopped by the Harp homestead on Wittenberg Road, Rush would fill him in on the latest in conspiracy theories over coffee. His place was a bachelor's lair, full of surprises; once he showed the flaneur a Thompson submachine gun he had just purchased. He liked to invest his money—at one time he owned the *Woodstock Times*.

A chubby, generous eccentric with a ready smile, he was always ready to come to the aid of those who called him. "Rush to the rescue" was his motto. All he asked of others was they listen to his theories. When asked how he was, his invariable answer was "supreme."

He carried on his "research" by telephone, which he would invariably answer, "Hello, telephone."

He died in 1982, and his friends threw a memorable memorial party in Town Hall with lots of dancing. (Rush loved to dance.)

One Summer Day
in Byrdcliffe

THE FLANEUR went for a walk in Byrdcliffe on a fine summer day in the late eighties, and here is some of what he saw.

Mount Guardian

HE MET AILEEN CRAMER in the old quarry that served as a trailhead. Cantankerous, opinionated, Aileen was senior member of the Woodstock Guild board that inherited Byrdcliffe from "Pete" Whitehead. For her, clearing the Mount Guardian trail was noblesse oblige. The flaneur followed her lead, and let her do the talking—it was difficult to do otherwise. She used the big clippers, and he picked up the cuttings and tossed them. They marked the spots that called for a chain saw, and it was still early morning when they reached the summit. They straddled the boulder, looking down upon Woodstock, and out over the green mountains that marked the borders of Ashokan.

"I wish it could remain like this," she sighed. "But it won't. Human beings spoil everything."

The Movie Star

THE FLANEUR WALKED PAST Bob Dylan's old house, and came to the Villetta, on Camelot Road across from the theater, where a bustle of activity indicated progress in preparing the first artists' residency summer program. He sat on the Villetta steps, and soaked in the sunshine. Then a familiar face blocked the sun with its own radiance. He drew a sharp breath of mild disbelief. Viveca Lindfors smiled down at him with the same smile she had given Errol Flynn in *The Adventures Of Don Juan*. She had come to Byrdcliffe to do a play, *The Passion Of Anna*, in the Byrdcliffe Barn, and he had interviewed her.

They hit it off when he said his favorite of her films was *The Damned*, directed by Joseph Losey, an apocalyptic science fiction film in which she plays a sculptor, one of the most convincing portrayals of a female artist he'd ever seen.

"I hope I'm not interrupting your thinking time," she said, laughing the way beautiful famous women do when they know a man would be bonkers not to be thinking solely of them.

The flaneur was no exception, being a movie buff, he was hypnotized, as if the giant figure on the silver screen had stepped from it to stand over him in his theater seat. They had talked easily during the interview, but that was professional. Now he was simply a fan, and he was tongue-tied. She had a question about taking a hike—it was such a heavenly day!—which he answered without offering to be her guide. Other movie stars came to Byrdcliffe because of River Arts Repertory's productions in the theater across from the Villetta, stars of greater magnitude, like Paul Newman, Treat Williams, and Joanne Woodward; but the flaneur, in his forties that summer day, had a crush on a woman over sixty he'd first seen on-screen when he was twelve. Then he has a chance to spend time with her, and he's too shy. Go figure.

After awhile he got up and walked slowly down the road to the Byrdcliffe Barn, where the Fugs were rehearsing. They would appear with Allen Ginsberg that evening. The barn was sold out.

The Fugs

TULI KUPFERBERG was standing outside the entrance to the barn when the flaneur arrived, talking with fellow Fugs Steven Taylor and Ed Sanders. Before the flaneur could greet them, Allen Ginsberg came out, blinking in the bright sun. It would be the flaneur's job to introduce them before a large crowd that evening. Ginszap, as Ed had nicknamed his old buddy, looked well for a man with liver cancer. Tuli looked frail. The Fugs were turning into the Fogeys, the flaneur thought. He had known Allen casually since being introduced to him by Ray Bremser in the sixties. He said he had to set up chairs for the concert, and Allen volunteered to help. They worked in silence for a while, and then Allen asked about the make up of the audience. "A lot of people still looking for the sixties," the flaneur told him.

Allen looked around at the signs for past and upcoming events: champagne and candlelight classical piano concerts, cabaret, special events. "It looks like a lot is going on right here," he said.

That night Ginszap and The Fugs took everyone back to the sixties. (Tuli fell off the stage, but was unhurt.) Byrdcliffe rocked.

Ghosts of Byrdcliffe

IT ONCE SPRAWLED across fifteen hundred acres on the hills above Woodstock, a Utopian art colony with an attitude. In the beginning it was run by its founder as his private crackpot kingdom. If he did not like you, you were not invited to stay and make pottery. His dream was of a self-sustaining colony, but he died still supporting it. His son sold off land to pay the taxes, and upon his death it was willed to the Woodstock Guild of Craftsmen, an organization too small to care for it properly—then and now.

Byrdcliffe Arts colony is a national treasure. It was, in large part, responsible for Woodstock's worldwide reputation, long before the Woodstock Festival was a twinkle in Michael Lang's eye. If all this is news to you, welcome to the party. Byrdcliffe is Woodstock's real claim to fame, unknown and unheralded by national media. It is even a secret to many Woodstockers.

In an effort to get the word out, the Guild was renamed the Woodstock Byrdcliffe Guild. Inelegant, but okay. Now comes a new brand, Byrdcliffe at Woodstock, which is not a place name, but rather a title for a gallery show. (By dropping "Guild" from the new name, the seventy-five-year history of the organization is ignored.)

The flaneur takes an interest in the effort to spread the news about Byrdcliffe because (here comes the full disclosure) he was the Guild's Program Director for ten years, wrote a book published by the Guild about Byrdcliffe, and formed and headed the Advisory Committees that were charged with attracting attention to the art colony. When Sondra Howell became the Guild's first Executive Director in 1982, she started the effort to revive Byrdcliffe.

A wealth of new programming brought attention and people to the colony in the eighties. Eager to be part of it, the flaneur thought nothing of walking there from his Glenford home on a spring morning.

In those days, River Arts Repertory was in residence at the Byrdcliffe Theater, staging challenging fare by playwrights like Mac Wellman, Janusz Glowacki, John Whiting, and Tom Stoppard. Actors of stature such as Treat Williams and Joanne Woodward, trod the dusty boards of what had been the colony's art studio.

One of River Arts' directors, Rob Thirkield, offered acting classes that the flaneur signed up for. Rob was quick to size up people. Before the flaneur knew it, he was drafted for a staged reading at the theater. Rob was quietly inspirational—and tormented.

There was always a reason to stroll the quiet Byrdcliffe roads. Sometimes on a Sunday afternoon the flaneur would help Woodstock historian Alf Evers lead a guided tour of the colony, one which might go on for twice the advertised time. Alf loved his subject, and he loved to talk. There was a good story for each building.

Another old-timer who could tell good Woodstock stories was Byrdcliffe caretaker Bert Van Kleeck. Bert told the flaneur about his friendship with his boss, Peter Whitehead, the son of the colony's founder. Both men liked to lift a glass, and once, while in their cups, Bert got so mad at Pete that he chased him down a Byrdcliffe road waving a butcher knife.

When Peter Whitehead died in bed in the founder's house, White Pines, his finances were in such bad shape that he couldn't afford to fix the leaky roof over his bed, so sheets of plastic kept the raindrops off. Whenever the flaneur thought of Whitehead's bequest of Byrdcliffe to the Guild, he thought of the king of Siam long ago. When the king disliked a courtier, he gave him a magnificent elephant. It was death to refuse the gift, but ruinously expensive to keep it.

The summer after the flaneur studied acting with Rob Thirkield, he attended a graveside ceremony for the director, who had jumped from a window. Overcome with grief, an artist friend threw a canvas into the open grave.

The Dancer With
Two Left Feet

THE FLANEUR WAS A SAUNTERER on the streets of his village, but he once had the ambition to become the world's greatest walker, following in the steps of his hero, Edward Payson Weston (1839-1929) another Ulster County resident with a screw loose.

Toward this end, the flaneur had walked across the state of Connecticut in one week as a warm-up. But he had gotten sidetracked, and then, twelve years ago, he noticed that his left leg had begun to drag ever so slightly. A visit to a neurologist confirmed his fears: Parkinson's disease, incurable, progressive, terminal. He thought of the Woodstock Parkies he had known—former town councilman Steve Knight had made a brave stand against "the palsy" until he got so shaky he had to sit. Edgar Leaycraft, town historian, Connie Goffredi....

The good news was that the flaneur's case was relatively light. No more hiking, not even serious walking; but he could still work, he could still boogie, although each day was like dancing with a new partner with two left feet.

Being something of an idiot, the flaneur is a congenital optimist, who had gone to Sunday philosophy school with Epicurus and he looked for the pony in the deepest dung pile. His glass was always half full, and spiked with more than a dram of determination. He was set on living a normal life, which meant concealing the symptoms of PD for as long as he was able. He did not want to be reduced to the label of his disease. Pity was for the pitiful.

The flaneur could accept, despite his youthful ambitions, the end of his long walks. He had gotten more pleasant mileage out of his legs than any ten people. The loss of his voice was more disturbing. His speech was becoming incomprehensible to those who didn't know him.

Now when he stumbled down Tinker Street, he began to notice the number of his fellow citizens, who, like him, were getting on with their lives while attempting to conceal the ravages of serious illness. He noticed—truly looked—as if for the first time, at the old and infirm, bravely pushing their walkers, and at the exhausted faces of those battling with affliction. Where before he had seen weakness, now he saw courage. It was a democracy of punishment to which he had been willfully blind.

He thought, when he saw his fellow sufferers, of their diseases. Cancer was the Great White shark. Everyone had lost someone to its bite, and despite the billions thrown at it, there was no cure. Yet most people would choose to fight the Big C rather than Amytropic Lateral Sclerosis, or Lou Gehrig's disease, a nightmarish monster of a killer that attacks the motor neurons of the brain and spinal cord, leaving the victim paralyzed.

Among them was his friend Larry Berk, whom he'd met when they'd helped Laurie Ylvisaker mount the three-year Woodstock Poetry Festival at the end of the last century. Larry was a poet, husband, and father, and the director of the Ulster County Community College Library. Over weekly lunches, Larry told the flaneur about his past, his fears, his hopes for his family, as you might unburden yourself to a stranger on a long flight. The flaneur listened with growing admiration for the courage of the doomed man sitting across from him enjoying his egg salad sandwich. He thought of revealing his own diagnosis, but couldn't bring himself to. His PD was not the equivalent of ALS. He would live, but soon his new friend would be no more.

The flaneur planned to live forever: so far, so good, he'd often said to himself. PD threw a monkey wrench into that plan. All he could do now was take it one day at a time—and stretch the hours until they snapped. But he was good at that; his life had been one long bucket list.

Something Larry had said stuck with him, like the words of a song he couldn't get out of his head. "You'll never regret the time you spent making love, or counting clouds. But I should have skipped more meetings." The flaneur had heard this sentiment before, usually from people who didn't know what to do with themselves after retirement. Hearing it from Larry was like a smack on the head from a Zen master.

Watching the faces passing him on Tinker Street, the flaneur looked for cloud watchers and love makers, but most looked clueless—sheep in green pastures of plenty. He resisted the impulse to run among them, shouting a warning about the wolves lying in wait, and the dancer with two left feet. He stopped himself from wailing, like Janis Joplin: "Get it while you can!"

Black Like Me

WOODSTOCK HAS ALWAYS had a small black population. One nineteenth-century census lists it at around fifty. In the thirties the KKK, protector of white citizenry, burnt a cross here just to show folks that they were on the job. Yet it seems strange, in pictures of Maverick Festivals, in all that gaiety to find not one African American face in the costumed cavorting crowds...perhaps they were not invited. Most artists in Woodstock then were communists, but even leftists can be racist.

When the flaneur arrived in Woodstock in the early seventies, he brought his five children. Two were black. There were a couple of minor incidents when they started school, but he was pleasantly surprised at how quickly they were accepted. It took him a while to realize that Woodstock was as white as Ivory soap.

Woodstock was a liberal town. At parties, if any bashing was done, it was of "rednecks." The word rubbed the flaneur the wrong way, but it was common currency among the politically correct. The word echoed other ugly words used to denigrate poor people who work with their hands: cracker, hillbilly, briarhoppers, etc. These can be fighting words in the Midwest. Growing up there, the flaneur had scrapped with many a school-yard bully until he realized it was futile to deliver a vocabulary lesson with your fists. When he began to call himself a hillbilly the taunting ended. African Americans had it worse, he realized, when he started to hang out in black jazz clubs on the wrong side of his segregated city. White cops separated him from his black musician friends. His first published writing was a letter to the editor protesting segregation.

After a lifetime studying race relations it seemed to him that despite hopeful signs, America remained irremediably racist. He wondered if there was anything new to be said, and thought of two aspects of the problem that were seldom discussed: class and language.

The flaneur had known some upper-class African Americans who had seemingly never encountered the color barrier. After all, even the prejudiced whites were not likely to fuss if Oprah Winfrey bought the house next door. In fact, he was aware of some black families that were of such refined pedigree, and had such educational and financial attainments, that they even looked down their noses at Barack Obama. The flaneur was certain that for many whites it was poverty and ignorance, not skin color, that made them haters. These same people turned their noses up at hillbillies.

In most communities artists are outsiders. They can't be trusted to buy the brand of reality the chamber of commerce is selling. Like African Americans, they are a minority, lonely figures in a closed communal landscape. The black artist Ernest Frazier must have felt doubly alone in his Saugerties studio; he spent a lot of time in Woodstock, where he exhibited in WAAM shows, and at the Kleinert Arts Center when Sondra Howell showed his large abstract paintings, which were heavily influenced by Basquiat.

Although the flaneur spent a great deal of time with Ernest, they were not close. Ernest made it difficult. He was eccentric—to a degree which at times exceeded what might be allowable even to an artist—and he had a speech impediment, but he was a handsome, often charming man whose dreadlocks seemed to dance about his head when he got excited about race. He stuttered. One Thanksgiving dinner Ernest was complaining about kids calling him names on the street. They were Puerto Rican, and he'd lost his temper and retaliated—but with a smile. "Guess what? They loved it. They even helped me carry my paintings up to a gallery loft. All they wanted was to get my attention."

The flaneur was intrigued. Except for auxiliary members of the PC police, no one had brought up the issue of language and race since the sixties stand-up comic Lenny Bruce had demonstrated how to wring the evil power out of racist words: use them. Say the offending word run-on, fast as you can. It's meaningless gibberish inside a minute. Bruce also reminded his audiences that in the heyday of vaudeville all the ethnic slurs were in constant use—before a Family of Man kind of crowd. The flaneur hated censorship, and doubted it would stop bigots from spewing their mindless venom.

Take the six-letter "N-word" for instance. Almost every sexual slang word could be found in today's magazines, but never the dreaded "N-word" unless it came from an African American. He had an idea. The flaneur's family had always been suspiciously dark, and both blacks and whites still accepted the antebellum rule of thumb that one drop of black blood in your veins makes you African American. A recent DNA test shows that the flaneur—pale face that he is—has much more than a drop of the sub-Saharan plasma coursing through him. He would henceforth categorize himself as black.

Or better still, he would be a r***n**k n***.

⊛ ⊛ ⊛ ⊛ ⊛

Otherness

⊛ ⊛ ⊛ ⊛ ⊛

WHEN THE FLANEUR lost his voice to Parkinson's disease, the irony did not escape him. If fate wants to mess with you, it often employs its fickle finger to rob you of an attribute you are proud of. There are over one million Parkies in the U.S. and ten million around the world, and each one of us has been robbed of something precious. The disease will keep subtracting from its victim until life itself is stolen. The tulip has been chosen as the symbol of PD, and sometimes when the flaneur allows himself to consider his loss, he imagines a giant garden where ten million tulips of all colors are in bloom—then, before he has time to appreciate the massive beauty of the sight, a great hand pokes down through a cloud and begins to clip....

We are our voices, we are what we say, the flaneur thinks. As a teenager, girls said he sounded a bit like Elvis. He thought he sounded more like a radio announcer. When he lived in New York, he read his poetry in libraries and bars. Looking back, he wondered if people clapped for his voice, and not his verse. It was a voice that could command order at a contentious meeting, caress a radio microphone, or entrance children at bedtime. He thought PD had left him his voice. Then he began to stutter.... Soon his radio voice was a memory. The trace of Elvis was long gone, but his Elmer Fudd imitation was Oscar quality: "wascally wabbit," he cursed, stumbling over his thickening tongue. Some of his intimates could figure out what he was trying to say, but most, including his Beautiful Wife, found it difficult. His handwriting was illegibly micrographic, his speech lessons inadequate. He was fu-fug flummoxed for sure.

Reluctantly, he settled into obmutescence, a state in which silence is golden. He was handicapped, but did not think himself so until one day he approached a stranger to ask directions, forgetting that when he opened his mouth, instead of words the squawk of an indignant chicken might issue forth. The man's smile froze. Uneasiness became fear, and then it was toot-toot-tootsie goodbye.... The man obviously thought he had a screw loose. The flaneur conceded that he had become a freak.

Could it be that the PD had drained his batteries?

One morning he went for a walk on Tinker Street before the stores opened. He couldn't forget the fear he had seen in the eyes of the man he had squawked at. It was a dark December morning on the Village Green. The occasional pickup truck passed, mostly town maintenance or highway. He came to the Green when there was serious thinking to be done–or a memory light had to be switched on. Since the Green had been the scene of so many community events, arrivals and departures, memories crowded his mind. He looked through them for the fear he'd seen.

It came to him. Thirty years before, he had taken a job caring for retarded people. (The current euphemism, he believed, was intellectually disabled.) He chose to call his charges innocents, because he disliked the popular American ideal of innocence. When people talked about protecting the innocence of children, what he thought about was society dumbing them down and keeping them powerless. His charges were truly innocent because they were completely powerless.

Sometimes he and other workers would take these innocents on field trips to Woodstock, where they hoped people would be more understanding of their peculiarities. Certainly a troop of innocents might disconcert those encountering them for the first time. Innocents were odd, without question. At one time they were part of the community, now they lived out of view in group homes.

They paraded down Tinker Street, holding hands, happy without cause except to be out in the sunshine, going for ice cream. Many who passed smiled kindly, but a few frowned and stepped back, avoiding contact, as if the strange noises and awkward gait of innocents might be contagious. The flaneur remembered seeing the same fear on the faces of whites in close proximity to people of color in the south. He saw it on television news in reaction to immigration. It was always "us" versus "them"—otherness was at the bottom of the conflict everywhere. The Internet and social media were driving people apart, inflaming the primordial fear of the other, the stranger, which is our legacy from the caves.

Now his shattered voice made him Other. He was handicapped. From now on, when he met someone new they would be responding not just to him, but to their own reactions to his handicap. Pity and fear and annoyance would mix, and cloud every encounter. He would be judged, as we all judge each other, not for what he could do, or who he seemed to be, but for his Otherness.

⌖ ⌖ ⌖ ⌖ ⌖

Woodstock South

⌖ ⌖ ⌖ ⌖ ⌖

TO GET TO WOODSTOCK SOUTH, fly to Mexico City and catch the next plane to León. The bus is cheaper and more comfortable, but the bus station is across town a half hour by taxi. Mexico City is huge, sprawled across the landscape like Los Angeles.

San Miguel de Allende was colonized by Woodstock artists long ago. There is a famous art school where Woodstockers have been teachers and students. A few years ago the flaneur flew down to the old colonial town to visit his friend. Stella Chasteen. Stella is a ceramic artist whose favorite artists are Bosch and Brueghel. She's a Scot who studied with Lucian Freud at the Slade School in London.

The flaneur arrived, with his usual impeccable timing, on the Day of the Dead, a part of Halloween Mexicans take very seriously. That evening, before dinner with Woodstock artists Alan Siegel and Mamie Spiegel, the flaneur and his hostess walked down a narrow street in which each house displayed a window exhibit celebrating the artfulness of death. It was a view into the national psyche. Perversely cheered by the skulls and coffins they'd viewed, the flaneur and Stella drank the excellent Mexican beer, Negro Modelo, and ate their bloody steaks with gusto.

Unsurprisingly, the conversation turned to the subject of the day. The flaneur told them of the strange and lonely death of Neal Cassidy, the Beat Generation figure Kerouac wrote about in *On The Road* as Dean Moriarty. He was found dead, of causes unknown, on the railroad tracks leading into San Miguel.

The next morning was hotter than usual in the mountains, so they drove to La Gruta, a swimming hole not far from the town. It is a natural grotto, entered by water down a long dark tunnel, a birth canal, from which you emerge into the fierce Mexican sunlight, refreshed if not reborn. (It was also a spa, so he discounted the easy symbolism.)

The Jardin (pronounced har-DEEN), smaller than New York's Washington Square Park, is the center of San Miguel. After lunch they claimed a park bench, and watched the town go by, from noisy balloon sellers to new mothers showing off their babies. The rowdy birds in the trees competed with the happy stridency of the mariachis and the rapid Spanish of those who promenaded past. As the days passed and he settled into the slow rhythm of life in paradise, the flaneur took stock of himself and his new environment. He looked for what Mexico had to teach him and decided that the lesson presented by Mexico was astonishment ... and time.

Time was an illusion, it did not move, he saw. It remained the same, while we moved through our lives. In this sense, the Mexicans were Aztecs. This revelation was as astonishing as watching the sunrise. He turned it over in his mind, and found no way to escape its truth. Woodstockers who lived in San Miguel warned him that Mexico was a trip, and now he began to see what they meant. Here were people who barely had two pesos to rub together who seemed happy; people who were called lazy by racists, who worked harder than Americans. He watched the sweepers, and the lines of a poem came to him: "At five in the morning, / In the garden beneath / The blue jacaranda / Where the peacocks scream / And the fountain refreshes / The riotous flowers, / I sweep the blue shreds of dawn."

The Jardin was always immaculate. One morning he was surprised to find an American newspaper left on his favorite bench. The bench gave him a complete view of the pink towers that rose above the neo-Gothic facade of Parroquia de San Miguel Arcángel. Someday he would enter the church. For now the towers were all he needed to ascend to heaven. He picked up the newspaper and felt dizzy. It was March 1997, and the news reported the suicidal departure from this dimension, possibly by UFO, of thirty-nine members of the Heaven's Gate cult.

Why was everyone in such a hurry? Heaven would call soon enough. He thought of the calacas, the tiny skeleton figures like us getting married, playing the guitar—they were both funny and sad, bustling about, forgetting the skull beneath the skin. He watched a sweeper in the distance, and another stanza of his poem came unbidden: "I sweep the drowsy scorpions / From the rumpled bed of morning / So the day is easy / And without apprehension."

As he walked the streets of San Miguel, the flaneur recognized faces that had disappeared from Tinker Street. Some of them had just moved their crafts shops south to San Miguel, while others had built new houses in the hills. It was becoming an American outpost, with a distinctly Woodstock edge.

One morning Stella told him she wanted to destroy some of her ceramics. The flaneur saw no flaw in their beauty, but she was adamant. The flaneur proposed that she give them away. So that afternoon they sat on his bench in the Jardin and watched as people stopped to look at her discards, which he had placed across the street with a sign in Spanish: free. Most passed by without looking. It was several hours before they were all taken, a lesson in humility. Or was there a deeper lesson to be learned? Thinking about time standing still, and the Heaven's Gate suicides, he knew that he knew nothing. "I sweep the crumbs from the picnics / Of the poor, so they will not seek / Second helpings of what they cannot have."

Staring up at the towers, it occurred to him that Woodstockers came to San Miguel for what they could not find at home: peace. He finished his poem.

"At five in the morning
No one is here to hold
The great bunches of balloons,
And the April rain has washed
Away the cantilena of the guitars
And the triumph of the bright horns."

Exiled from Ashokan

IF YOU ARE AN AMERICAN, you are probably a nomad, willing to pull up stakes for a job opportunity if you're young, often more than once; if old, you head for warmer climes when the snow falls. If you're lucky, however, you find a place where you feel just right, and you call it Home. You don't mind getting away for a while on vacation or business, but too long away, and you begin to feel deracinated. Rootless.

The flaneur has been away from home since late October, and he is seriously homesick. It should go without saying that he misses his wife, his friends, and the amenities of home, but he also finds himself missing Ashokan, the landscape we share, in a way he never had before.

This makes sense, since it was the landscape as seen from Route 375 that he first fell in love with, and has spent over forty years walking in and writing about. He feels like the mythological giant Antaeus, who derived his strength from his contact with the earth. "Exile" is a big word usually reserved for writers banished by governments, but displacement from a beloved landscape may carry, for some, the weight of exile. (The new nomads won't understand the feelings of some local Woodstockers forced to leave their native ground in search of work.)

What happened to exile the flaneur is quickly told: a fall, a broken hip, hospital time, and then recuperation at his daughter's house in Dedham, near Boston, where he doesn't have to climb stairs. Dedham is a lovely small town, but there's something missing: mountains. In over forty years the flaneur has not been out of sight of Overlook for so long. And the great reservoir, where is it? It mirrors the universe for him. At home, all the roads he has walked in all weathers have imprinted themselves in his cellular structure. The roads here don't recognize him when he pushes his walker over them. The trees are strangers. Even the snow falls the wrong way. The flaneur could not tell you the names of nearby rivers, or even point to the four directions. All he knows is that Boston is not far.

The trouble with travel—especially tourist travel—is that you see only what's in front of you, an empty stage set of surfaces. You can't see what the native sees—the story attached to each building, street corner, and swimming hole. It's like a sixth sense about their homeplace that makes their experience of it incalculably rich. Compared to Fifth Avenue, Tinker may look drab to a visitor, but an inhabitant's associations bring it to colorful life.

A walk through downtown Dedham takes you past interesting buildings—courthouses, an old movie theater, a grand old Richardsonian library—but since the flaneur is an alien here, it's eye candy, without emotional resonance. Only time can change this.

He finds himself thinking of walks still to take, sights to be seen and written about in Ashokan. To fall in love with a landscape is a lucky thing. The flaneur dreams of leaving his house in

Glenford once again and heading up Ohayo Mountain to a view point where he can drink in the waters of Ashokan.

The beauty of this view is always worth the climb. The flaneur studies how the water moves, and how birds move over it. He remembers taking his kids fishing there, and intimate picnics on the shore. They went there weekly for many years, and then after September 11th they stopped. The reservoir was closed, and by the time it reopened they hadn't the heart to go back to what they loved.

His favorite example of the power home landscape can have is that his friend Bill Pachner who says he bought his land on Ohayo Mountain because the view it offered reminded him of his childhood home in Moravia. He has spent his long life recreating that view. Perhaps for some, love of a particular landscape is in the genes. The flaneur's family is from Kentucky, where they always look up to the mountains. Once a hillbilly, always a hillbilly....

In the broadest sense we become what our surroundings make of us. Looking up to mountains and out over broad expanses of water brings humility into our arrogant lives, and perhaps, at times, awe.

⊠ ⊠ ⊠ ⊠ ⊠

Strolling with the
Memorial Day Parade

⊠ ⊠ ⊠ ⊠ ⊠

THE FLANEUR STROLLS to the music of a different drummer;
by definition, he does not march. But he's so fond of the Woodstock Memorial Day Parade, and so eager—after a long, hard
winter and interminable spring rains—to greet summer that he
arrives early on Saturday morning at the newly renovated Woodstock Playhouse, the traditional staging area for the parade. He is
met by his friend Stella Chasteen, like him, a parade enthusiast.
After years of watching the parade together they are curious to
see behind the scenes. But there's not much to see.

The shiny red fire trucks are lined up, and floats promoting
Little League await squirming Little Leaguers. Five bagpipers
limber up their odd instruments. Town supervisor Jeremy Wilber
stops to chat about his career as a novelist. Actor Dean Schambach
holds a bouquet of balloons aloft. There is a feeling of calm—obviously parade organizer Kevin Verpent has things under control.

It's warming up—soon it will be hot—so the flaneur and his
companion decide to find a patch of shade up Mill Hill Road. On
the way they pass Sam Magarelli, who is passing out flyers about

Woodstock Volunteers' Day in August, and county legislator Don Gregorius, who tells them his Tinker Street antique store will be closing because he lost his lease.

The old benches in front of Catskill Art Supply are gone, a small but significant loss to town amenities, but there is a stone perch outside the Woodstock Frame Shop. Although announced for noon, the parade is typically thirty minutes late. Sure enough, at half past they hear faint music; and peering down Mill Hill, sight the parade coming up the hill: in the lead are teenagers tossing flags, stepping high to the music of the Onteora High School Marching Band, followed by Little Leaguers on floats tossing out candies and balls. The crowd applauds the kids because they love it and we love them, and the fire fighters because they have earned our gratitude.

Although the flaneur is not a fan of the combustion engine, he enjoys the classic cars town notables drive, especially an old black-and-white shoebox-on-wheels called a Metropolitan, which Stella thinks was made by Ford. (Actually, it was the product of an Anglo-American partnership and was produced in the fifties.)

The Veterans for Peace squad carry signs protesting the harsh treatment accorded

PFC Bradley Manning, the Wikileaks whistleblower. (Even My Lai killer Lieutenant Calley wasn't forced to stand naked all day in prison.)

The flaneur reflects on the peace movement, thinking that every soldier who's seen combat is, perforce, a veteran for peace, and the irony that if it were not for late-developing brain chemistry which makes it difficult for young men and women to assess personal risk, there would be no one to fight wars. While the flaneur respects people who militate for peace (and peaceniks are among the fiercest people he knows) for him it comes down to the simple fact that war is part of what makes us human. If we didn't like it, we wouldn't do it.

What the flaneur likes most about the parade is the chance to see his fellow citizens outside their normal context: Mike from Woodstock Hardware, for instance, looks very impressive in uniform. Other than in a true emergency, this is the closest one can get to seeing the faces of real-life heroes.

The feeling in the air is celebratory. Everyone is up because it's warm and sunny, the beginning of summer. Jogger John cavorts past on the sidewalk, masked and bare-chested, playing Pan. (Although at sixty-seven he's in good shape after decades of constant motion, it may be time for John to keep his shirt on.)

To keep up with the parade, they walk in the street and cut through the town parking lot. It is a pleasure to trod the irregular bluestone sidewalk past the cemetery, and to recall a time not that long ago when all the town's sidewalks were of native stone.

They stand outside the cemetery fence opposite the flagpole with several hundred people. Above them looms Overlook Mountain like a mother watching over her children. It is a long program moderated with aplomb by Terry Breitenstein, and it gives the flaneur ample time for reflection. There is a benediction, followed by speeches by politicians. Retired town supervisor Jeff Moran tells a story about an ancestor who had enrolled in the Union Army at fifteen, as a drummer boy. The flaneur thought of his own Kentucky great-grandfather, who'd joined up at sixteen, and lost a leg at the Battle of Lookout Mountain.

Is there anything more American than Memorial Day? It grew out of the Civil War, apparently begun in 1868 by freed slaves in South Carolina, and a little later in New York State by Union Army veterans. Called "Decoration Day" until after World War II, it didn't become part of a three-day weekend until the sixties. Now it is our national day of remembrance—a day when cemeteries buzz and brighten with the visits of the living, who bring flags and flowers. It is the day that opens the door on summer, glorious summer. After the parade the firefighters will party, and barbecues will be fired up across the nation. The flaneur thinks there may be no better way of forgetting nightmares than to commemorate them.

When the Pledge of Allegiance is recited, the flaneur holds his panama over his heart, and notices with some dismay how many men do not remove their hats during the ceremony. The flaneur knows that years from now what he will remember are two singers. The first, Abby Hopf, belts out "God Bless America" a cappella. She's no Leanne Rimes yet, but give her time—the blonde angel is only four, and so pocket-sized she is carried off stage.

But for the flaneur it is Don Haberski's rendition of the national anthem that is the highlight of the ceremony. Unlike many celebrity singers who open sporting events, Don can carry—and do honor to—a difficult tune. He was in great voice, and his singing gave new meaning to the military phrase "shock and awe." Who knows the talents hidden in the bosoms of people we see every day? Memorial Day reveals small wonders about our community.

Rifles are aimed, volleys are fired, and little boys scramble for spent shells. The flag is raised; taps is played, sad and haunting. Like Kabuki theater, the same tape unwinds. The faces change, but the ritual does not. What had begun as a gesture of gratitude to veterans has become the quintessential American day. (Strangely, the flaneur has heard no mention of the three wars we are embroiled in now.)

The flaneur and Stella leave, walking down the center of Rock City Road, which is closed to traffic.

"That was just about perfect," the flaneur said. "It's Woodstock at its best," agreed Stella.

Tales of Two Cemeteries

The Woodstock Cemetery

THERE ARE PEOPLE who don't like cemeteries. They see no point in visiting departed friends who can't hold up their end of a conversation, and those whose real estate has shrunk to the dimensions of a single bed. They cannot live reflectively, anchored in the earth, but must be fully engaged in interactive busyness, as if they could put off the Reaper until they are ready to go along with him hand in hand into the dark. In contrast to these ostriches, the flaneur is drawn to cemeteries. They are oases of quiet in a pell mell world. The flaneur has traveled to Woodlawn Cemetery in the Bronx in search of the final port for Herman Melville, and to Père Lachaise's crowded precincts in Paris, looking for the cork-lined coffin of Marcel Proust. The flaneur visits his ancestors by climbing a remote hill in Lawrence County, Kentucky. Growing up in Appalachia, he was surrounded by the small funerary hills of the Mound Builders.

The flaneur has always loved walking in Woodstock Cemetery, so when his friend D. J. Stern (née Boggs of Boggs Hill), recently retired Woodstock Library Director and local history buff, said that she wanted to visit that community of the departed for archaeological reasons, the flaneur volunteered to accompany her. They parked at the top of the cemetery on a road that separates the oldest graves from the newest, next to the stone of Jane Neher Earley Keefe—three resonant names in the town. Delicate asters peeped up across the green lawn.

Visiting a necropolis offers, among other melancholy pleasures, the opportunity to preview eternity. This is what forever looks like, at least on this material plane: a quiet hillside raked by a chill wind with a weed whacker buzzing in the distance, and a splendid view of Overlook Mountain.

D.J. pointed out the graves of many people she had known, her shadow looming over their monuments. As she took photos with her Polaroid, the flaneur noticed Ludwig Baumgarten's stone. Once Woodstock's own Wyatt Earp, "Lud" seemed like a one-man police force in his time as constable. On the flaneur's first weekend visit to Woodstock the tall lawman gave him two tickets. Lud was everywhere—he even admonished young men for going bare chested.

Down a row of stones sleeps a man whose name has much to do with Woodstock: Martin Comeau, 1880-1971, the lawyer who served as the town's civil defense chief in World War II. His house and land are the centers of town government and recreation.

As if in a scene from *Our Town*, D.J. pauses before certain graves and recalls their occupants. An important one is Andrew Chandler Lee, born 1938, who died in a hunting accident in the fifties. Few who recreate in Andy Lee Field know that he was so popular that it was named in his memory.

There is Fred Ohls, responsible for Woodstock Elementary's first school bus, and down the road from Mr. Ohls sleeps Rick Danko of The Band, illustrating the odd juxtapositions in the democracy of the dead. (A cemetery plot is no more expensive than a month's rent.)

Nearby is the most famous site in Woodstock Cemetery, Catherine Van De Bogart's elm tree grave. Catherine died in 1820, the victim of a cruel husband, (or so the legend says) and an elm tree supposedly grew from her heart. Today her tombstone is propped against a lilac bush.

The caretaker of this necropolis is Shay Cocks, a handsome, raffish young Charon wearing a camouflage jacket and an earring in one ear. Shay volunteered to show them the oldest graves, those of Woodstock's Revolutionary veterans: George Happy, who died in 1833; Joseph Fox 1749-1827, captain of the Continental line; Captain Phillip Bonestill, 1751-1834, first Woodstock settler. Their stones are cracked and nearly illegible because they are marble, and not native bluestone.

The flaneur asked Shay about the size of the cemetery. He guessed it was about fourteen acres. He chased kids away at night, but it was easy for them to hide in all that space. He found needles and glass pipes. Vandalism is a problem: "They not only knock over tombstones, they pull the spear points off the ornamental fence and throw them into the grass, which breaks the mower."

The flaneur and D.J. drove down to the front and walked past more recent graves, passing that of D.J.'s mother, Mae, whom the flaneur had known as a smiling presence in a wheelchair, and D.J.'s grandfather, Henry Wilgus, who ran the general store in High Woods for many years.

Then they came upon Rush Harp's monument. It was a shock. They both had known the rotund Kennedy-assassination buff with a big heart who called himself "Rush to the Rescue" for the many times he saved his friends from scrapes and breakdowns. A memorial party after his death filled the town hall in one of the best parties the town had ever seen. The shock was learning that Rush was only sixty-one when he died, according to his stone. They'd thought of him as old when he crossed the Styx. Now they had lived past his cut-off date. Rush had died young!

As if to mock their dismay, the writer Eli Waldron's marker nearby reminded them of Eli's advice about the Grim Reaper: "Everybody Knows, Everybody Goes."

The figure of the Grim Reaper looms over cemeteries. One of the reasons they are quiet and usually empty is the fear factor. Only rebellious teens will go to a boneyard by night.

When the flaneur's family lived on Simmons Drive, he walked home on moonlit nights mindful of the spirits behind the fence, and he whistled to keep his nerve up.

Shay Cocks tells the story of a man who didn't want to see the tombstones as he passed up Rock City Road, so he paid to have a line of trees put up to hide them. The trees grew tall, but unfortunately for this donor, new graves were dug in front of them close to the fence.

Closest to the fence is the marker of Woodstock's first town supervisor, Elias Hasbrouck. It is embedded in a boulder for good reason: someone stole it, long ago, and it was only returned when a Woodstocker happened upon it in Manhattan. For the most part, cemetery visits peak on Memorial Day, a holiday apparently started in 1868 after the Civil War to honor the soldiers who fell in that internecine bloodbath. For years the flaneur has attended the ceremonies at the cemetery after the annual Memorial Day parade; although he considers himself a citizen of the country of Ashokan, he places his hand over his heart and gets misty eyed when taps is played. But he wonders, standing there, if the people around him understand during their brief once-a-year visit the true importance of a cemetery to a town. It is where everyone ends up, after all, and it might be said to contain the spiritus loci of Woodstock—the sempiternal memories of all those we have loved and lost. May the earth rest gently on their bones.

The Artists Cemetery

THE SMALL NATURAL AMPHITHEATER that is Valhalla for generations of Woodstock artists was spotted with small American flags on the bright May morning when the flaneur led Will Nixon for a visit. It was the week before Memorial Day, and many of the artists interred there were warriors once.

In contrast to the town cemetery across Rock City Road, the Woodstock Memorial Society Cemetery Association—the official name of the Artists' Cemetery—seemed like an exclusive private club. The flaneur could imagine the departed rising at cocktail hour for a great incorporeal bohemian party—although the way the graves are arranged, cascading in an orderly fashion down the steep hillside toward the Whitehead sepulcher with its della Robbia centerpiece—is more suggestive of a college classroom.

Ralph Radcliffe Whitehead, the principal (he had the money) founder of the Byrdcliffe Arts Colony, would have been pleased, in his aristocratic English way, to preach the gospel of art to this congregation.

Wandering among the elegantly presented stones on the slant hill, the flaneur mused about the funerary practices of artists, in particular the wish to be remembered for one last work of art: a tombstone.

He was particularly struck by the beauty of those that bore only the engraved signature of the artists. They reminded him of the only other artists' cemetery he had visited, in Springs, on the south fork of Long Island. There, the poet Frank O'Hara's stone bears his signature and his beautiful line, "Grace to be born and live as variously as possible." Nearby is the grave of Jackson Pollack, also identified with his signature.

As the flaneur examined stone after stone, he found himself mischievously tempted to review them. After all, artists live for critical attention. Perhaps they would enjoy some posthumous comment.

Such a review would have to begin with the opinion that the stone of another Byrdcliffe founder, Hervey White, is second only to Whitehead's. It is a starkly modernist beauty, the artist's name runs vertically in a stripe down the center of the stone.

"What strikes me," Will said, breaking into the flaneur's reverie, "is how many wives outlived their husbands."

It was true! The twin slabs for another Byrdcliffe pioneer, Carl Olaf Eric Lindin, and his wife Louise Hastings Lindin, are aesthetically united by engravings of Viking ships, but she buried her husband.

Then there are Milton and Sally Avery. Long after Milton passed on, the flaneur was in Sally's studio in Bearsville looking at her work. When he opined that he liked it better than her husband's, she shot back, "Then you're a fool." No doubt; but the flaneur stuck with his judgment.

Belmont and Phoebe Towbin: twin stones featuring engravings of hands touching and lines of poetry by Yeats.

Sid and Polly Kline were old-school journalists. Polly wrote press releases for the Woodstock Library when she was well into her nineties. The flaneur served on the library book committee with Sid and admired his intelligence. Sid was a regular at the old Pub when the flaneur overheard him challenge his fellow drinkers to name the Seven Wonders of the Ancient World. (They did.)

Among the other notable stones the flaneur admired were those of Walter "Bud" Plate (whose widow is living), a fine painter; Henry Morton Robinson, author of the bestseller *The Cardinal*; and Robert Starer, whose mate, southern author, Gail Godwin, found a true home in Woodstock.

The flaneur had known Robert, and seeing his grave struck a chord of sadness: so many souls death had undone. Depression threatened on a bright morning. Here is where we all end up.

But the flaneur took some deep breaths, and counted his blessings with each inhalation. He's still vertical, for today at least, he told himself. The best way to honor these departed artists was to bask in the sun while he could.

He thought of the advice of a wise third-century BC Chinese master, Yang Chu: "If anyone cares for one hour's blame or praise so much that, by torturing his spirit and body, he struggles for a name lasting some hundreds of years after his death, can the halo of glory revive his dried bones, or give it back the joy of living?"

It may be said that how we honor our dead is an indication of what kind of society we are. It struck the flaneur that the best way to honor those who have preceded us into eternity is simply to visit their graves. Perhaps the dead get lonely and lament our neglect of them.

⊗ ⊗ ⊗ ⊗ ⊗

River Arts Repertory
Remembered

⊗ ⊗ ⊗ ⊗ ⊗

IT SHOULD BE RAINING, the flaneur thought, as he joined the little band of mourners at graveside in the Artists Cemetery. It was overcast, but lightning and thunder would have added dramatic accompaniment to the interment of an actor and director who had jumped from a window in Manhattan just days before he was to be married; a man still young, talented,wealthy, and charismatic.The gods of the theater must have had urgent need of his talents, to trick him into such precipitous flight. It was August 1986.

The remains in the box that were to be fed to the earth were those of Rob Thirkield, who, along with director Larry Sacharow and Pulitzer Prize-winning playwright Michael Cristofer, was responsible for bringing world-class professional theater to Woodstock, presenting, through the eighties, plays by the most challenging contemporary playwrights.

The work of River Arts Repertory in the Byrdcliffe Arts Colony was followed closely by the flaneur, who had once dreamed of becoming a playwright, but had gone no further than seeing one of his one acts produced Off-Off Broadway.

As he stood on the fringe of mourners, half-listening to what people were saying about Rob, the flaneur fought off his growing anger and tried to concentrate on his encounters with Rob and River Arts. He looked around and saw many faces absorbed in making grocery lists, and a tall man he recognized as Calvin Grimm, a prize-winning painter of abstract landscapes, pushing his way through the list makers bearing a large canvas. Calvin made it to the grave's edge just as the coffin was being lowered, and, with a grand gesture befitting a Viking funeral, tossed his offering into the grave. Rob would carry a representation of the mountains around Woodstock with him on his voyage to the Blessed Isles. Whatever emotion possessed Calvin to make this gesture, the effect was electric. This was the drama that made the burial ceremony memorable.

The flaneur recalled what Rob had taught him. The flaneur had told himself that he'd left his playwriting ambitions behind because he couldn't abide the egos of actors, when the real reason was that he hadn't the knack required to write plays. A good actor searched for the truth of a role within himself; acting was not about ego, but honesty. Most of us lie. The flaneur wanted to learn how to stop. He had warmed to Rob. Now he suspected Rob was dead because he had lied to himself.

River Arts was imbued with excitement and glamor. The flaneur admired the company's artistry, ambition, and professionalism. During its fourteen-year run at Byrdcliffe Theater, it produced plays by Tom Stoppard, John Whiting, and Edward Albee, among dozens of top-drawer choices.

Famous actors walked Byrdcliffe lanes memorizing lines. When Joanne Woodward came to play in Chekhov's *The Seagull*,

Paul Newman tagged along with her and hung out on the Village Green sipping a paper-clad Bud. Larry Sacharow was good looking and smooth as a matinee idol. He ran the company day to day and was the face of River Arts at its fundraising events.

The best known of the three directors was Michael Cristofer, who was a triple-threat talent as playwright, director, and actor. He had gotten his own way for so long that his look was dark and demanding. The flaneur would have cast him as Bosola in Webster's *The Duchess of Malfi*, a favorite character.

These three were bishops in the ancient church of theater. Their house of worship was indeed ancient. Built at the turn of the twentieth century, it had seen art exhibits and concerts, as well amateur theater. Old timers still remembered the Turnau Opera, and it was there that the flaneur had staged five major publishing conferences with his friend John Baker, editor in chief of *Publishers Weekly*.

The company rented the theater (and the Villetta for housing) from the art colony's owner, the Woodstock Guild.

At that time the Guild was property rich, but cash poor. The Guild needed its rental income. At a lease-renewal meeting Larry Sacharow presented an idealistic plan that would not only have lowered the rent, but would have made the two arts organizations partners in presenting theater in Byrdcliffe. The flaneur liked the idea, but representing the Guild, his charge from the board was to insist on the rent. So he said, "The Guild is not an eleemosynary organization." End of negotiations.

A Citizen of Ashokan

ON A WARM LATE SUNDAY AFTERNOON in mid-October the flaneur lay sprawled on a boulder atop Mount Guardian, studying, from the Hudson River on the east to the mountains of the west, that patch of the northeastern Catskills known to most as the Woodstock valley, or, even, Catskill Park. It was to be his new country. He would name it Ashokan, which supposedly means "place of many fishes." He didn't care about the word's authenticity—he liked the sound of it, and the great reservoir it named. He removed his boots, and a cool breeze tickled his bare feet. A fly landed nearby and rubbed its legs together. It was the sole audience to the words he spoke:

"I pledge allegiance to the mountains and waters of Ashokan ... and to the great lake that is its center. I offer my friendly respect to all beings that share this bioregion, from humans to moles in the earth, and my enmity to those who would despoil it."

He had to smile at this last, imagining himself holding off a gang of frackers with fine words. "Well, why not?" he asked aloud. "After all, the American colonists didn't have much more when they started." The fly flew, after buzzing him in solidarity.

He watched a turkey buzzard drift in the breeze that was tickling his toes and forced himself to think about politics. His musings drifted loopily, like the turkey buzzard.

In graduate school in the sixties his leftist friends made jokes that often began with the phrase "comes the revolution...."

The revolution they expected never came. The center held.

The flaneur was willing to bet that Americans would never protest the status quo without a strong leader—et voila! Conan the Barbarian grabbed the mic. The people who follow him are mad as hell, and they are not going to take it anymore—"it" being the cozy way the top one percent rake in eighty-five percent of the profits of prosperity while the rest of us must make do with what farmers bluntly call "hind tit." These days it was hard to escape politics.

With Conan promising to rid the country of Mexican rapists and conduct diplomacy like a ten-ton gorilla with tactical nukes as sidearms, he was likely to tromp a woman few liked or trusted. That the greatest country in the world could produce only these two to lead it was a jaw dropper. Fear and frustration now ruled. A voice from the past whispered in his ear, "That's the problem with democracy: when anyone can be president, you're taking a big risk."

Woodstockers were talking about hightailing it to Canada. Politics was making life miserable. The flaneur felt the need to do something, but what? Then it came to him: He would start a country, and ask his friends to join him; instead of heading for the border, come to Ashokan! The flaneur liked to think big, but this was Cinemascope big. And the beauty of it was that nothing had to be done—no money exchanged, no armies marched. The imagination would do the heavy lifting.

Was he crazy? He asked himself this question every morning, and so far had given himself a "pass." This idea was preposterous, but he couldn't stop himself. As he saw it, the Republic of Ashokan would exist solely in the minds of those who chose to claim citizenship. Since physically Ashokan would occupy the same space as the Woodstock valley, Ashokanites would continue to live and work in the "real" world of Ulster County, but in their imaginations—their personal virtual reality—they would be operating on a higher plane. Just as the fictional Yoknapatawpha County exists more vividly in the minds of generations of admirers of William Faulkner's fiction than does the factual Lafayette County around Oxford, Mississippi, so would Ashokan become the dominant reality in the minds of its citizens. Changes in how things looked, how things were done, would be arrived at by agreement. One month you might notice ground being cleared for a new (and unnecessary) mall, and the next time you pass, see sheep grazing in that spot. No politicians had been lobbied, no officials schmoozed; the owners of the property had decided that a mall did not fit with their vision of Ashokan, and so it would go, citizens choosing the Platonic ideal over the material "reality." Those entrepreneurs looking to make a quick buck would complain of conspiracies, but he thought that citizens—not consumers, not homeowners, not tax payers—would make the right decisions about Ashokan because it was their home.

The flaneur thought his idea was easily grasped, but he knew there would be resistance on Tinker Street, and derisive squeals from the Comeau. (This was Woodstock, after all.) If voters became citizens who got together and did the right thing without coercion, what role would government play? The flaneur imagined that town fathers would be kept busy if they concentrated on Woodstock and didn't spin wheels debating passionate resolutions about national affairs outside their purview.

When he told his friend Walking Will Nixon that he was going to start his own country, Will gave him the sharp appraising once-over you give friends you suspect of going around the bend, and commented wryly, "Start-ups are expensive."

Surprisingly, some of the most vociferous reactions came from those who said they would head for the border if Conan won. They told the flaneur that he was in denial, and that he had to face the fact that the country was turning fascist. The fly was back to buzz in his ear.

His thoughts turned to the psychology of denial, and he dozed off. Wasn't everyone "in denial"—about death, for instance?

Would it not be better to ignore Conan for four years and tend our own gardens? Better to grow roses than kick against the pricks?

His cold feet awakened him. As he pulled on socks and boots he found himself looking for the fly, but his interlocutor had apparently buzzed off. The flaneur remembered that flies see through thousands of lens in their eyes. Could they see into the future? He looked out over the country he had created, and hoped that it would last.

Michael Perkins is a poet, aphorist, essayist, critic and novelist, who has published over fifty books. His prose and poetry have appeared in national periodicals from *Mother Jones* to *Nortre Dame Review*. He divides his time between Dedham, Massachusetts and the Hudson Valley.